The Magical Realms of Elfin

Answers to Questions About Being an Elf and Following the Elven Path

The Silver Elves

Copyright © 2017 The Silver Elves, Michael J Love and Martha C. Love
All rights reserved.

ISBN-13: 978-1981559855

ISBN-10: 198155985X
Printed in the United States of America by CreateSpace

Without limiting the rights under the copyright reserved above, no part of this publication may be reproduced, stored in or introduced into a retrieval system, or transmitted in any form or by any means (electronic, mechanical, by photocopying, recording or otherwise) without the prior written permission of the copyright owner and the publisher of the book.

Dedication

We would like to dedicate this book to our elven kin who have asked us over the past four decades many thought provoking questions about the elven path and who have explored the realms of Elfin with us, and with special gratitude to our dear sister Ileådryn (Sara Hotchkiss).

"Men would ask, did the chicken or the egg come first, while elves would wonder if elves or Elfin came first, but we know the answer, we arose together, born of each other's magic."
—The Silver Elves

Table of Contents

Introduction 1

Chapter 1:
"First Questions" About Elves 3

    What does it mean to be an elf and
follow the Elven Path? 3

    Is the Elven Way a religion? 6

    What does it mean to awaken to our true Elven Nature? 7

    What is the difference between Elfin and Faerie? 8

    How do The Silver Elves relate to Tolkien? 10

    How do I know what sort of elf I am? 12

    How do I become a Silver Elf? 14

    Could there be an elven cult? 17

    Is there anything that all elves have in common? 18

    If you are elves, why don't you have pointed ears? 20

    How do you know if a person is an elf or faerie
or pixie or whatever? 21

    What are fae? 23

    Are elves Indigos? 25

    Do people who believe they are elves suffer from
Schizotypal Disorder? 27

Are people who think they are elves and faeries crazy? 28
Is there one term for elves, faeries and otherkin? 30
Elfin, Faerie or Elfland? 32
What's the difference between elves and faeries? 35
Who are the half elves? 37
Are there really diminutive Fae Folk? 40
Are elves related to angels? 42

Chapter 2:
Elven Magic 45

What is Elven Magic? 45
What is rainbow magic that the Silver Elves
often speak about? 46
Do elves do ceremonial magick? 48
Do elves do ritual magic? 51
What is the difference between "Magical Thinking"
and superstition? 53
Do elves curse people? 57
What do the Silver Elves think of Using
Reiki in their Magic? 59
What is the Orb of Healing? 61
Are all elves mystics? 63
How do you give Elven Blessings? 65

Chapter 3:
More About Who the Elves Are 67
   How can an elf be born from a man, pixie, etc.? 67
   Are there any real and absolute physical characteristics of being Elven? 70
   Is being an elf a matter of blood of genetic heritage? 71
   Are we born to be elves? 73
   Are all elves tall? 75
   Are all elves thin? 76
   Are elves healthier than other people? 78
   Do elves age less quickly than normal humans? 79
   Do elves sweat? 80
   Are all elves white? 82
   Are elves always androgynous? 83
   Do elves have enhanced senses? 84
   Are elves hypersexual? 86
   Do elves have facial hair? Are elves ever bald? 87
   Is there a point at which one is too old to be an elf? 90
   Are elves politically liberal? 91
   Are Elves Nature Spirits? 93

Chapter 4:

Elven Awakening *95*

    How important is the Awakening compared to Perseverance of the Elven Way? 95

    What are the different modes of Awakening? 98

    Once an awakened elf are you always an awakened elf? 100

    What is a Reawakening? 103

Chapter 5:

How The Silver Elves Are Alike and Different From Other Spiritual Practices *107*

    What's the difference between elves and Pagans? Do The Silver Elves follow an "Elven Faith?" 107

    What's the difference between elves and witches? 111

    Is Christianity incompatible with being elves? 113

    Can elves be atheists? 114

    Do elves believe in past lives? 116

    Do elves interact with teraphim? 118

    Do elves interact with Genii Loci? 120

    Are the Elves the same or different from the Djinn? 122

    What do the elves think of the Illuminati? 123

    Are elves related to Devas? 126

Is the sphere of Netzach specifically related to Elves?............128
Are Elves New Age or different? 129

Chapter 6:
The Past and Future of Elves *131*
How far back in history do elves and the original
"Elven Faith" go?..131
Are elves from Pleiades? 133
Who came first, elves or faeries? 136
Is it the Elf Star or the Faerie Star? And who
first adopted the seven-pointed star as the Elf Star
and what does it mean? 138
Are the legends true that say elves kidnap people? 140
What will happen to us if humanity destroys itself?...........143
Are elves the people of the future? 144

Chapter 7:
How Elves Relate to Other People *147*
Why are elves born into the normal world? 147
What say the elves about living in the world
of the unawakened? 150
Do you tell all people you meet that you are elves? 151
Where do you find kindred fae? 153
How does an elf find friends?...................................154

How do you deal with individuals who pretend they are more spiritually evolved or more magically adept than they really are? 155
Do elves hate dwarves? 158
So if elves are born elven, are orcs born to be orcs as well? 159
Is it necessary that we elves be forever in conflict with orcs, goblins and grimlens? 161
What do elves feel about transgender individuals? 163
Who are the Elf Friends? 165

Chapter 8:
Elven Lifestyle *168*

Are elves vegetarian? 168
What's the elfin view on wearing fur? 171
What do the Silver Elves think of people who wear fake wings to be like faeries? 173
What do the Silver Elves think of those who wear fake elf ears? 175
Are there specific elfin holidays that the Silver Elves celebrate? 176
How do elven communities govern themselves? Do they have kings and queens? 178
What do elves think of body modification? 180

Chapter 9:

The Language of the Silver Elves:

Arvyndase (SilverSpeech) *183*

    Do The Silver Elves speak Arvyndase (SilverSpeech)? 183

    How do The Silver Elves create the elf names
    they gift to others? 184

    Does knowing a person's true name really give
    you power over hir (him/her)? 186

    What do you do with your elf name? 188

Chapter 10:

Oracles of The Silver Elves *191*

    What oracles do the elves use? Part 1: Tarot 191

    Beside the tarot what other sort of oracles
    do elves use? Part 2: I Ching 194

    What oracles do elves use? Part 3: Runes 196

    What oracles do elves use? Part 4: Geomancy 198

    What oracles do elves use? Part 5:
    The Elven Star Oracle 199

    What oracles do elves use? Part 6: Miscellaneous 202

    What oracles do elves use? Part 7:
    Magic the Gathering 204

    What oracles do elves use? Part 8: Necromancy 206

Chapter 11:
Other Miscellaneous Questions About Being an Elf 209
    Does iron burn elves? 209
    Do elves have green thumbs? 212
    Do elves prefer gardens or wild places? 214
    Do Silver Elves only exist in *Dungeons
    and Dragons* books? 216
    What would you say to an elf in prison? 218
    Do Elves really follow their Dreams? 219
    It is true that Seelie Elves cannot lie? 222
    Do the elves love poetry? 223
    What is the difference between Elven and Elvish? 225

Chapter 12:
The Silver Elves Books 229
    What book by The Silver Elves should I start with? 229
    What book of yours is best if I'm interested in …?
    Part 1: Magic 232
    Part 2: Elven Philosophy 234
    Part 3: Elven Lifestyle 237
    Part 4: Divination 239
    Part 5: The Elf Queen's Daughters 242
    What about the accusation that the Silver Elves books
    are a mish-mash of cultural appropriation? 245

**Are all The Silver Elves' books unique
and original writing?** 248
Why do you use the royal "we" when writing? 250

About the Authors *253*

Introduction

We Silver Elves have had many questions about being elves and the elven way posed to us throughout our 40+ years of following the elven spiritual path and sharing with the world that we are elves in human bodies. Recently, we have noticed that these inquiries and questions have greatly increased because it seems that more and more people are becoming interested in knowing about elves and the elven community. Many of us like to think that there is a spiritual Awakening of our kin beginning to occur worldwide, and this may certainly be the reason for all the recent curiosity about elves and the elven way. Of course, too, Tolkien's romantic descriptions and understanding of elves made popular by recent movies (*The Lord of the Rings Trilogy* and *The Hobbit*) have certainly contributed to the growing numbers of participants now joining in the modern elven community, and with a surge in social media this community is becoming more accessible by the day to the general public and sparking more and more excitement and reflection about all things elfin.

We are always happy for this communication, dear sisters and brothers, and do encourage those interested to feel free to contact us with your comments and questions. We decided to put all of the questions posed to us both through the years and recently about being elfin together in one book for anyone who needs a convenient yet thorough and easy-to-read resource to explore their questions about who the modern elves are and about the elven way or elven spiritual path. Most often, a person has questions as one tries: to decide if one is ones'elf an elf or is some otherkin; to understand what it means to be an elf and how one might know of one's elfin nature; to understand one's experience of having an elven Awakening; to determine how elven magic is alike or different from that performed by other spiritual groups; to decide which of our Silver Elves' books to read on various interests about the elven way, our magic and about being elfin (we have 41 books now, so people often need some guidance on which to start reading first or to explore a certain elfin interest); and to learn about how elves live and relate to mankind and otherkin. So, if you are curious about modern elves, particularly about The Silver Elves (as we do not speak for all elves as elves are quite a varied and independent folk), then you will surely find many of your questions answered within this book.

And please feel free to contact us if you have other questions either through our email at silverelves@live.com or on Facebook under the names Michael Love (Zardoa of the SilverElves) or Martha Char Love (SilverFlame of the SilverElves). Also, please enjoy our website at: http://silverelves.angelfire.com, where you will find some of our Magical Elven Love Letters posted for you to read, a page dedicated to all about how to be gifted an elf name from our beautiful elven language Arvyndase, our Elven Tree of Life Eternal (a sort of choose-your-own-adventure to explore your magical nature), and descriptions and sample passages from our 41 books on elven magic and enchantment and the elven way. We also invite you to follow our two blog sites, where some of the questions in this book are also posted and where you will find that we will continue to write articles about the modern elven movement, elven lifestyle, elven magic and enchantment, and the elven way: see (https://silverelves.wordpress.com and https://thesilverelves.blogspot.com).

Chapter 1:
"First Questions" About Elves

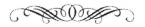

> We have included in this chapter the questions that people often ask us first when they are introduced to the idea of there being modern elves manifest in human bodies, when our newly found kin feel that the spiritual call within is beckoning them on to examine whether they themselves may be an elf, and also when normal folk experience a growing curiosity about elves. As we pointed out in the introduction, we find that more and more people today want to know about who we elves are, they want to know if they might themselves be an elf and if so how would they know, and also what is the elven way or path.

What does it mean to be an elf and follow the Elven Path?

This is like the questions, what does it mean to be a woman, or what does it mean to be a man, or what does it mean to be a human being. All of which can be answered in innumerable ways by various individuals and still never encapsulate the entirely of the question. What does it mean to be an elf? Well, first it means that we are spirits who have chosen to manifest as elves. That, first and foremost, is the most important thing because being an elf is always about choice. While one may feel that as an individual sHe had no choice but to be born as a man or a woman or to this or that race, these elves think that we are elves principally because we have chosen to be so.

The thing is, however, there will certainly be other elfin who feel that they were born as elves and had no other choice but to be elves. And while we disagree with this point of view, we cannot help but recognize their right as elves to believe this if that is their wish. Usually, however, we tend to think that people believe this because they wish to assert their essential elvenness in a world that almost continually seeks to deny their elven being and ridicules them for even daring to think that they are elves. In saying that they were born elven without a choice in the matter, they assert their right to be elves no matter what others may think. This is the same dilemma that confronts gays (who are often faerie folk) who feel they must assert that they are gay by nature because of those who say instead that they are gay by choice and have no right to be. But, from an elven point of view, it doesn't matter if they are gay by nature or not, they have every right to choose to be gay, just as we have every right to choose to be elven.

Still, it seems to us that we choose to be elves, which is to say, we choose to manifest as elves or not. We could, for instance, choose to deny our elven natures and hide among normal folk. Many of us have tried to do this and a great many of us have failed for while we can sort of pass among them, most elven never quite feel comfortable among the normal folk and they in their turn are never quite comfortable around us entirely either. They usually feel they can trust us once they get to know us, but they are never quite sure what we are (which is something strange and wondrous) and if we told them they wouldn't believe it anyway. At the same time, the choice to manifest or not as elves is ours. In many ways, it is really about whether we accept ours'elves or not.

In a certain sense this question: what does it mean to be an elf, is really about individuals searching for some definition of elvenness that they can compare thems'elves against. We could say an elf is this or that and they could see if it fits them and thus know if they are elven or something else. But the problem with this is that elves, being the unique and individual beings we are, never fit comfortably into set categories and no matter what you might say about what it means to be an elf, you'll probably find some elf who says: 'well, not this elf'. And again, how could we deny them their right to pursue their elfinness however they may define it. Elfin and Faerie are vast and there is room for everyone in it. Those who don't accord with our sort of elfin nature will find their way to another part of Elfin. But none are denied and none are rejected—not by Elfin and not by these elves. Only the individual hir own s'elf can deny hir entry into Elfin. Only the individual can deny and reject hir own elfin nature. The most we can say is, they are different elves than we, and that is surely true of nearly all elves, even our most beloved. The principle that opposites attract holds true in Elfin as well as the rest of the Universe.

But in another sense, the meaning of being an elf depends upon the elf hir own s'elf. 'What does it mean to hir?' is the essential question. So the question really is: what does being an elf mean to you? And only you can answer that question and mostly you can only do so by your behavior, your actions, your magic. What you say is not nearly as powerful or telling as what you do.

For these elves overall, being elven means creating a world of wonder and magic where we can be together in love forever with our beloved kindred. Beyond that, it is really up to each one to make of Elfin what sHe will.

~

Is the Elven Way a religion?

The path of the elven is not religious in any way but is rather a spiritual quest of the individual's effort toward the development of each one's own s'elf and soul, which is to say one's connection to the rest of the Universe and the Divine Magic from which all things spring. In other words, the miraculous nature of our existence.

None-the-less, many folks upon discovering that we are elves jump to the conclusion that we must be a cult of some kind. This is particularly so when we have an elven community no matter how large or small.

This assumption is, of course, understandable because quite often when individuals in modern society encounter a group with strong philosophical, spiritual or religious beliefs they are part of a cult. But at the same time, this jumping to the conclusion that we elves, individually or collectively, are part of a cult is really just laziness on their part, an unwillingness to actually discover what we are about. However, that just tells us that they are not elven or not ready to relinquish their enculturated social views enough to truly examine their s'elves or us and that we simply have to respect. You can't drag people kicking and screaming into Elfin. The results would be unsatisfactory for them as well as us. All we can really do is understand their reluctance and hesitation, and nurture them as best we may and, in most cases, move farther and further along our own path and leave them to theirs as best they can understand it. If fate or destiny should bring us together again, we will sprinkle another touch of stardust upon them (without them realizing it ever happened) and await the fulfillment of the magic.

∂

What does it mean to awaken to our true Elven Nature?

When elf and faerie folk first awaken to their true natures, they often attempt to define that nature in very limiting ways, often saying that there are only five types of elves or eight types of fae folk, or otherwise narrowly delineating elfin nature, such as proclaiming that elves don't kiss or that no elves are gay or other such nonsense.

Naturally, elves and fae folk who are more advanced in their understanding of their s'elves reject such limiting declarations. However, we come to realize in time that these attempts to limit the nature of elves aren't really a reflection of an outward expression but actually an inward one. These individuals in attempting to limit all elves are really seeking to define and discover their own elven nature. They are not really saying, even though they think they are, that no elves kiss but rather that they come from a tribe of non-kissing elves, or that no elves are gay, but that they thems'elves are not.

Once one realizes that all these outer projections are truly an expression of the individual, all becomes clear and one can smile and acknowledge their efforts to declare their own natures while avoiding any sense of being personally limited thereby. For it is the right of every elf to define hir (his/her) own nature and this right cannot be abnegated nor abridged by any other.

❧

What is the difference between Elfin and Faerie?

Faerie is a realm that includes all otherworldly beings and places. When we use the word Elfin we mean by that a place that is particularly the realms of the elves and those kindred who are directly related to us, the pixies, faeries, brownies, leprechauns and others. Elfin then, to our minds is a bit more refined than Faerie. Tolkien referred to Faerie as the Perilous Realm and it can surely be that. It is like a dream that can be either very pleasant or a nightmare in which one has absolutely no control whatsoever over what is going on. In fact, for most folks, this realization that we lack control over our lives, that the world is much vaster than we often let ours'elves realize and that at any moment nightmarish things may happen, is the lingering possibility of the nightmare that lurks just out of the corner of our eye as we step into Faerie.

This is not to say that all of Faerie is dangerous. But like nearly any city in the world, in Faerie there are areas where it is unwise for certain individuals to go, that are dangerous areas except for those who reside there and sometimes even dangerous for them, and the danger can spill over at times, invade what seem to be the more comfortable and secure and protected neighborhoods. Elfin on the other hand, to our minds, is less like a dream where one has no control, and is more like a lucid dream, where one can encounter the dangers that may exist in an intelligent and conscious way.

Faerie is a vaster Realm than Elfin and you could say that Elfin is an elegant, safe and wonderous neighborhood in Faerie. In a certain sense, one might say that Elfin is more like a garden, while Faerie is the vast wild spaces filled with lions, and tigers and bears, oh, my ... But in saying that, it doesn't do Elfin justice. There is still a wildness to Elfin but it is a less dangerous wildness, a more secure and protected wildness. It is a sanctuary of the Elfae people where they may be thems'elves safe from most of the dangers of the world. If we used the card the Fool in the Tarot to represent Faerie, the Magician would represent Elfin for in Elfin the most dangerous things are the Elfae ours'elves who will not abide harm to those we love.

In some ways, it is like the difference between being insane and being crazy in a wild, weird, eccentric and loving way. We elfae are all crazy pretty much, but we are not insane. We generally function fairly well in the world or as well as the world will let us do so, for the world seems determined to drive nearly everyone insane, while we elves merely go wild and crazy instead, retreating into the secret realms of Elfin that are inaccessible to normal folk who deny their very existence.

So, while Elfin is a garden, a garden of our creation, it is a rather wild garden, filled with color and life in profusion where we allow all the plants to pretty much go mad and grow every which way they choose and we do the same. But it is not so wild that you have to be on guard at every moment, ready to defend yours'elf at an instant's notice, for we are here with you, beloved, and Elfin protects us all. And if you wish to have a more dangerous adventure, well, you can always journey deep into Faerie and take your chances, and if you wish to attempt to bring healing to a mad, mad, mad, mad normal world, well ... good luck with that but remember you can always come back to Elfin where you may be healed from any contagion that occurred through contract with that insane world, which thinks it is right about nearly everything and is usually so very, very wrong.

How do The Silver Elves relate to Tolkien?

Most elves in the modern age love Tolkien and his works, both the books and the movies, and in particular we love the way he portrayed the elves. He took us out of the purely ephemeral and etheric, the realms that most folks don't even believe exist, and brought us back into human bodies as we had been of old, as we were often portrayed by the Scandinavian peoples. This is not to say that there aren't elves who are more etheric in nature, but that we who are currently manifesting in human bodies appreciate the recognition of our state and our identity.

Tolkien even indicated, by his marriage of Aragorn and Arwen and of other couples, which is to say by the idea that there were half-elves, such as Elrond, that we are of one species with mankind, as terrible as that is to contemplate for some elves. For we can interbreed between our races and here we mean race not so much as it is used in the modern sense, to be peoples with strong physical differences, but in the old sense when people spoke of the German race, the French race, the Jewish race, the Chinese and Japanese races and so forth. That is the idea of race that has some sense of physical differences, but more subtle usually than today, and a greater emphasis on cultural variations. For our own part, however, we Silver Elves define race more from spiritual differences than physical ones.

We remember Arwen, one of our sisters of and a founder of the Elf Queen's Daughters, standing in her living room in the home that they had that had a seven foot high elf star painted on the outer wall, shouting out, "We love Tolkien. We'd like to canonize him," which is to say make him a saint. And that is how most elves feel about him. He is an elvish saint, both as a writer who helped illuminate our culture and from what we know of him as a spirit, as an individual soul, as a person.

And yet, as much as we love Tolkien and his portrayal of us, his works, while good even great surely, are only a small part of elven culture and while some would wish to define us and limit us to his view of our kindred, the vast majority of elven, even while adoring him, don't wish to be limited by his views. We are glad he shed a light upon our culture but it is light that is only coming from one direction.

For one thing, he doesn't have our wonderful faerie cousins in his works, or our beloved pixies, nor our gentle brownies and so many other kinds that exist in our realms, gnomes and elven kin of such a myriad variety it would be impossible to mention them all here. We faerie folk have permutations and variations that cannot be listed because they are ever evolving and growing, new ones coming into being at the very moment we write this and more at the moment you read it.

Ours is an inclusive culture and we would deny none who are sincere and who truly wish to discover their elven or otherkin nature. Those who set themselves up to judge whether someone is worthy to be our kin or of our people are not of our kind. We embrace all those who come to us and know that while some may come doubting the veracity of our identity, as long as they are elf friends, true friends to the elves, our magic will transform them and they will be touched by our elvish starlight magic whether they realize it or not. Or culture is infectious. It instigates mutations in others and if they hang around us they will inevitably become who they truly are as well, and we shall bless them in their genuineness and love and adore them as our very own.

ಶ

How do I know what sort of elf I am?

Knowing who you are is an age old question. The quest for the true s'elf is a lifelong and in fact lifetimes long pursuit, taking place over many lives. In a sense we are ever coming to know ours'elves, or lose touch with ours'elves in the case of some folks, and at the same time the s'elf is not something that is stationary or static but in its'elf ever changing and transforming, which makes the quest even more challenging. We elves are protean by our very natures. We are starlight manifesting into forms and matter.

In the process of finding and becoming our true s'elves we often decorate our beings with the attire of the definitions of the world, taking on or rejecting and sometimes accepting and then rejecting or vice versa, this or that version of ours'elves, just like people trying on various clothes before going to a party.

In this process we often seek various ways of looking at ours'elves, finding those things that seem to accord with our inner nature, and also going through the process of accepting or declining those definitions of ours'elves that are offered to us or projected upon us by others. Thus these elves frequently have kindred write to us and tell us that they are uncertain of what sort of elf or fae they may be, hoping that in some way we might be able to tell them. But while we may offer suggestions if someone really insists, it is not our decision to make but up to each and every elf to decide for hir own s'elf who sHe really is.

This is, in part, why we created our book *The Elven Tree of Life Eternal: The Magical Quest for One's True S'elf*, set up in a way like a choose-your-own-adventure book, that has a process that one can use for discovering for one's own s'elf what hir elfae true nature really is. By the way, this process is also offered for free on our website at http://silverelves.angelfire.com where one can explore the Elven Tree of Life Eternal and discover much about one's true nature.

There are however others who are willing, even eager, to tell someone what sort of elf sHe may be. It is just not our thing. There are even some who make that determination arbitrarily based upon a person's birthday and astrological sign. And there is surely nothing wrong with this but alas, we regularly get requests for elf names from individuals who've been told that they are this or that type of elf using this system who just didn't feel it is so. It just didn't accord with their inner feelings about thems'elves. And that is the point really. Only you know, deep within, what sort of elf you really are. Only you can say what sort of elf you may be and more than that only you can, by your actions, which is to say by your magic, make that inner feeling come to life in reality.

For in the long run, it is only by trusting your own feelings, your own inner attractions and inclinations as an elf, that you find your way to your true s'elf and thus to the inner realms of Elfin. Others may suggest aspects of elfin character to you but only you know for certain. For, in truth, if you are letting others define you, then you are not really an elf, or surely have yet to truly awaken to the truth of your own true nature, which is that you have the power to direct and guide your own destiny, particularly to decide who you are by what you do. Be true to your s'elf and all will flow from there. And a star will shine upon your brow touching the elf in others and blessing all whom you encounter with the grace of Elfin.

How do I become a Silver Elf?

People sometimes ask us how they can become a Silver Elf, meaning that they wish to join our group. Alas, we don't actually have an organization to be joined. We are in fact a family of elves and elfae, of otherkin and elf friends and are not an organization at all. If you wish to join us all you have to do is communicate, hang out and be our friends.

Of course, we use the name Silver Elves as our nom-de-plume, our pen name for our books, but we also use it to signify our rather ad hoc and often spontaneous gathering of myriad kindred that like to hang with us for a time. People often call us up and say, "We're coming," and if we are at all available we reply, "Great." Thus Silver Elves is not actually a specific type of elf but an indication of these elves who do and have gathered together, without really trying, elves, gnomes, pixies, rangers, brownies and various other sorts in community living situations, for adventures, as well as distant kindred and elf friends. We suppose we could call ours'elves Rainbow Elves, and that would convey the idea better, but we like calling ours'elves Silver Elves. And we never set out to be a miscellaneous gathering of elfin; it just happened.

If people ask we often tell them we Silver Elves are the elves of woodland, moonlight and starlight and that just about covers it as well. Being a Silver Elf is as easy as being our friend and joining us is as difficult as it is to get from wherever you are to where we are. Not to mention, or really also to mention, we don't really have the wherewithal to take care of other folks. People who hang around these elves pretty much have to take care of their own s'elves. We're doing good just keeping our own humble lives and situations together.

And currently, we happen to live in a very small apartment, in a very wonderful place, although we have lived in bigger apartments, condos and houses previously and nearly always collected others around us and often living with us. This is not something we ever did intentionally, just something that seems to happen naturally. Elf kin come. We accept them for however long they wish to be with us, which is usually until they find their soulmate or establish some romantic connection elsewhere and go off to pursue that relationship. Somehow without trying and without doing anything in particular to put people together, elfae find others around us, or through us or just because of the magic.

We know that our lack of organization surprises some folks and confuses others. People often assume that we are a cult of some sort or at least some worldly structured group. But Silver Elves organization is some form of oxymoron. And it is not that we can't organize some sort of elf frasority (combining the words for frasority and sorority), but we just don't bother to do so, or maybe don't wish to do so, and truly are much happier to just let things happen naturally.

However, we're always open to making new friends and certainly ever happy to connect with and hear from old ones. All sincere folk are welcome and they don't even have to be elves or even otherkin, one just has to be open-minded enough to understand or accept that we are elves and leave us be to be so. And we will accept you for whatever you wish to be and in harmony we shall move together into the future dancing with joy and in celebration of our friendship.

So, do you want to join us? Of course, beloved, we're always here for you and ever have been and though in time we will surely pass on to other realms and dimensions, we will carry you forever in our hearts and minds and until we meet again in love, be ever blest.

"Things are never normal in Elfin, but they are what we call elven typical, which means strange and unusual but quite fine."

—Old Elven Knowledge

Could there be an elven cult?

Cults are almost always centered around a charismatic personality, an inspiring leader and we elves are not immune to such personalities. In fact, being charismatic is nearly a description of elves in general, and we surely find such individuals intriguing. Even when we are introverts, we tend to have a certain charisma about us. The fact that we are magical folk and radiate elfin/faerie magic often means that people are both attracted and repelled by us, which is to say they find us fascinating, while being uncertain about us until they actually get to know us. This is especially true of those who are paranoid and suspicious anyway and prone to superstition.

For our own part, while we enjoy charismatic folks and are in fact fascinated by geniuses of various sorts, and surely would find a powerful elfin figure enchanting, we are seldom fooled for long. If that individual is really all about hir own s'elf and fails to foster the individuality in the kindred, we would soon fade from hir, just as sHe (she/he) in centering everything on hir own s'elf instead of nurturing the elves around hir would become more and more distanced from Elfin and the source of elfin magic.

Some of us, perhaps most of us, may be fooled for a short while, but only a very few will be taken in for a long period and those we expect have some karmic duty to fulfill in doing so, some inner need of their own as well as a need to serve the charismatic other, whom we assume and hope in time will overcome hir own inner emptiness and begin to accomplish the task of encouraging our beloved fae folk, which, after all, is the true purpose of such power.

So, while cults may develop among the elven, they are unlikely to last very long, we are simply too eccentric, unique and diverse as individuals for it to be otherwise.

❦

Is there anything that all elves have in common?

The thing that elves have in common is our love of all things elven. Beyond that, and a propensity to do and be interested in magic in various forms, particularly in enchantment, which is the chief magic of the elves, what we have most in common is that we are nearly all of us eccentrics in some way. Thus what we have in common is our differences.

This can be somewhat frustrating for those who are eager to define us in more precise ways and particularly frustrating for those newly awakened elven who wish to have some sort of guideline to base their elven nature upon. But really, what they need to base their exploration into Elfin most upon is their own s'elves, their own love of Elfin and their individual nature without projecting that nature necessarily upon every other elf.

It is understandable, of course, that those who feel a kinship to elves and Elfin wish some guidance in the quest of their true natures, particular since the world is ever trying to tell them to be something else, something acceptable to the masses and the masters. But, alas, all we can really tell them is to be true to their s'elves, to be tolerant of others, and most of all to be the best elves they can be as best they are able to understand it their own s'elves and thus to be ever ready to change and evolve, to adapt and develop their s'elves in this never ending quest toward 'elf realization.

A lot of awakening elves get their ideas of the nature of the Elven from Tolkien and surely he is a good source for while he didn't understand us entirely, he did give us some very advanced and wise models of elfin being. Not perfect beings, surely, but often advanced spiritual beings whose nature is a good thing to aspire toward.

And numerous folks attain their ideas of elvishness from the ancient lore, either directly or through modern works of fiction based upon this knowledge. Always, they will be drawn to what appeals to their own natures and this is natural and, in its way, wise as long as one doesn't assume, as unfortunately some do, that the way they understand elves to be is the way all elves are or must be. That will never work out because elves are not only incredibly diverse but also ever diversifying. As our numbers grow, as more and more individuals awaken to their elven natures, the more myriad shall our people be. But if we don't exercise and promote mutual tolerance of all save that which is intolerant, then we have surely lost our way and will wander out of Elfin and back into that world that is so eager to judge everyone by its own standards and seeks to pressure each and everyone to conform.

We are elves and although we honor our ancestors, we are not bound by the past. And while we find much in the world amazing and the works of modern writers who speak of us sometimes fascinating, we are ever creating our own styles. We are neither parrots nor cuckoo birds. We are the flocks of Elfin and we each have our own song that we sing in harmony together.

If you are elves, why don't you have pointed ears?

Many people ask us this question. We, like most elfin folk, love pointed ears. Alas, most of us don't have pointed ears, although there are some who do, and wish we had. Some of us put on prosthetic ears, as some faeries put on faerie wings, and some of us have even undergone body modification to make our ears pointed. That's how much we love pointed ears.

To those who don't believe in elves, or at least don't believe we are elves, the lack of pointed ears is proof that we are not. But then, those individuals have a basically materialistic viewpoint of the nature of the Universe and we have an energetic and magical viewpoint (as one would expect from a magical people), which is to say we don't judge people by their looks but by their actions. It is not our appearance that makes us elves, but living by the principles of Elfin that we call the Elven Way (see our book titled *The Elven Way: The Magical Path of the Shining Ones*).

Still, we love pointed ears, just as faeries love wings, and witches and magicians, wizards and warriors love the accouterments of their being. You don't have to wear a pointed hat to be a witch, or carry a staff to be a wizard; being a wizard, witch, magician or whatever is about doing magic, not having a particular look. But when you love the look, as we do, why not embrace it?

༄

How do you know if a person is an elf or faerie or pixie or whatever?

Unlike some folks, these elves for the most part don't tell people what they are. We don't generally say, "Hey, you are an elf," or whatever. We tend to let people tell us what they are and usually we elicit this information by revealing our own elven nature to those we feel might be open to it and then seeing if they respond and how. Often, if we tell someone, "We're elves," and they are otherkin of some sort, they will reply saying, "I am, too," or "I'm a faerie," or as was the case with our daughter, "I'm a faerie elf."

This wasn't always true. Early in our awakening, we used to tell others that we liked or were attracted to that we thought that they were elves, too, and surely there is nothing wrong in doing so. It's just that, in most cases you tend to draw out the same sort of response, which is the revelation of an individual's true elfae nature or association whatever that might be.

We particularly remember one instance where we encountered a young woman of our acquaintance very shortly after we had been awaken by the Elf Queen's Daughters (see our books the *Elf Magic Mail* vols. 1 and 2 for their writings) and told her we thought she was an elf. She immediately replied that she was, in fact, a dwarf, which was something we had not suspected at all. However, this let us know that it is not our opinion of what others are that is important but their own understanding of their magical s'elves. Ultimately, whatever we may think they are, only their own aspirations matter and we have simplified and clarified things buy letting them tell us what they are instead of projecting our conceptions upon them.

This does not mean that we don't have opinions concerning certain individuals. We see folks that we think are elves, or faeries of pixies, trolls or whatever and we base this mostly upon their actions, their magic, their behavior, although their appearance sometimes plays a role as well.

We have occasionally come upon someone who looks like a leprechaun to us but when we tell them so they often say something like, "Someone once told me I looked like a leprechaun when I was on the bus." Or as is so often the case with leprechauns, who tend to be a bit cagey, you'll get an answer that is essentially, yes, without them directly saying so, but that's leprechauns for you.

But again, what is really important to us and in the long run to them, is what they truly wish to be in an Elfin Faerie world, if anything at all. Do they have a place there? Do they wish a place there? Our opinions are just that, opinions and not necessarily any more valid than anyone else's opinion. But a person's actions, hir magic manifests hir being and that cannot truly be denied although there are those who would attempt to do so.

And, of course, there are those who think they are one thing, such as an elf, but haven't really penetrated to the depth of what it means to be an elf, often projecting the ideas gleaned from stories written about us by those who aren't elven, or continuing the habits and carrying the baggage of their life in the world not only upon their own conception of Elfin but attempting to project them upon us and thus to limit the rest of us as well. But of this we have little concern. For we are elves and thus they cannot restrict us with their notions. And if they are truly elfin, they will learn in time what that means for them as well as developing a tolerance for what it means for us. All that we can do in the gentle time is set an example for them by being the best elves we can be.

ॐ

What are fae?

Others may have different definitions but when these elves use the word fae we mean to encompass most of the inhabitants of Faerie. This, of course, includes the faeries themselves, but also pixies, brownies, fee, fey, leprechauns and nearly every other manner of faerie folk, including the Shining Ones, the Tuatha de Danann, the Sidhe in their various forms and many others. Even we elves are fae in our way. And naturally, we include the merfolk, the selkies, the sea sprites, the wood sprites, the sea nymphs, the wood nymphs, the dryads, the centaurs, the satyrs and many other folk, which in that sense would also include Tolkien's Ents. How about hobbits? Are they fae? We'd think so, but a very brownie like fae, a very homebody sort.

The question is, however, at least for us, do we include some of the denizens of the darker realms of Faerie, the Unseelie folk, the trolls, orcs, goblins, grimlens, giants and others of darker sorts? Honestly, we don't know. We don't wish to exclude them, unless they wish to be excluded. We are related to some of them both by blood and marriage from long ages past. They are our kindred even if they are the sort of folks one is sometimes embarrassed to admit that one is related. And remember that certainly not all of the folk of the darker realms are evil. And while we don't tend to share the view of humanity as a whole that many of these folk have, nor their propensity to prey on others, as is the case with some of them, nor even with their religious, social or political views, nor their views on gender and the place of women in society, nor their prejudices concerning other races, we are willing to share a family meal with them in elfin frasority and kindreth. We are cousins, after all, even if it is just kissing cousins, and we are surely not inclined to kiss them in most cases.

And that's the point really, we never exclude anyone who wishes to be a part of Faerie and makes the effort to attune to that vast and wondrous realm. We surely could not exclude them from Faerie itself, but neither would we exclude them from our own hearts and understanding of Faerie. Only those who do not wish to acknowledge Faerie are excluded from it. But really, when it comes down to it, each must decide for hir own s'elf whether sHe is of the fae or not.

If some goblin, for instance, came up to us and said, sHe was not fae, we'd accept that as fact. On the other hand, if another goblin came up to us and stated that sHe was fae, we'd accept that as well, thinking then that we had encountered two different types of goblin, the fae and unfae. This, alas, has never happened, but still it is possible.

We don't present our definitions as absolutes, merely as indications of how we are using a particular word, phrase or term. We believe it the right of every person and every people to define they own s'elves or selves, but it is also their obligation in doing so to live up to those definitions as best they are able. Calling ones'elf an elf, doesn't make one elven, but living one's life as an elf, does. At least, this is true in the realms of magic and Elfin and Faerie, and they are in the long run the only realms that really matter to us.

So what do you think? Are goblins fae? How about hobbits? We are curious about your opinion. Let us know your point of view.

ҨӇ

Are elves Indigos?

We can't speak for all elves, but we expect that most elves feel a certain kinship with the description of Indigo Children. In fact, most of us were Indigo Children before anyone came up with that term. We also usually relate to being called Star Children, Space Gypsies, and even Freaks when used in a positive fashion. We are the Children of the Earth and Stars, the Moonlight, the Sun light, the radiant trees of Elfin, the Sea Shine and nearly any description of people who are magical in a positive way and surely the unusual and eccentric tends to appeal to us. We are the Ancient Folk, the Wyrd Folk, the glimpsed out of the corner of your eye people.

We are also quite okay with the idea that we are pixies, fae, brownies, Sidhe and various other otherkin descriptions. Although, Therians as a type of otherkin often see themselves as being different than elves, some of us elven, because of our shapeshifting abilities and our talent for inhabiting animal bodies in our shamanic trance magic, as well as having totem animals, are not beyond thinking of ours'elves as being elves, Aelfar, and Therians as well.

That's the thing about we elven. We tend to be very flexible and adaptable and easily relate to any others that we like and are quite adept at seeing ours'elves in others and perceiving the link and connection between us. You could call us Friends, for we surely are to all those who sincerely wish to be friendly, and that would do as well.

We are the Children of the Age that is Dawning and the Age that is yet to come. And we are the Children of Magical Ages that have passed long ago (see our book *Liber Aelph: Words of Guidance from the Silver Elves to our Magical Children*). Ever and always we are the twinkle in your mother's eye and the sparkle of your father's smile. We are the spark that ignites when soul mates meet for the first time. We are the laughter of children heard in the distance. The melody that comes from some unseen source in the forest. We are your own true s'elves calling out to you and it really doesn't matter by what name you call us. It only matters that you know that you are loved and guided and we will greet you when you step into Elfin with our arms wide and a smile upon our faces.

And it doesn't really matter what you call us, beloved, as long as you are calling us with love.

"For the elves, courtesy is considered a weapon that is even greater than a sword or a bow."

—*Old Elven Saying*

Do people who believe they are elves suffer from Schizotypal Disorder?

Certainly some therapists seem to think so about those who proclaim to be elves or otherkin, but really this is more of a social judgment about our failing to conform to traditional societal norms and values than it is an indication that those who believe they are elven or otherkin are schizotypal. Schizotypal Personality Disorder is a personality disorder that is seen as being related to schizophrenia and is sometimes called a schizophrenia spectrum disorder. It is generally thought that schizotypal behavior is characterized by a pattern of odd, eccentric feelings, actions, perceptions, and that the nature of this disorder significantly interferes with the person's ability to function in the world and relate to others.

Well, most elves do fulfill this description at least in part. And in fact, we quite often embrace most of it, since in our observation the vast majority of individuals in society who are afraid to do anything that doesn't conform to peer pressure are at least extremely stressed and often exhibit neurotic behaviors. The key here is that having a Schizotypal Personality Disorder significantly interferes with one's ability to function in the world. And in most cases, we elves get along with others well enough, are happier and function much better than most of the perpetually angry, complaining, and disgruntled individuals that seem to compose much of the world's population. Our ability to move through this world and function in it successfully with a peaceful soul, indicates that our belief in magic does not mean we have such a disorder.

This is not to say that there are no elves who suffer from this or other disorders. Surely, this is the case. Most of us were raised in an insane world where hoards of individuals insist on having more babies despite the population explosion, that pretend that global climate change is a myth, and that this or that god will beam them up at the last moment right before he (it's almost always he, isn't it?) launches the apocalypse. So if some elves are a bit crazy, we are pretty clear as to why this is so. This world tends to drive people insane. Just look around you.

Yet, surely not all of us are nuts (we'll explore this a bit more in the next section), and those of us who aren't, who are merely following our own unique path and creating our personal elven myths, are also seeking to help and heal those who are still suffering from the traumas of the world. We have not entirely succeeded as yet, but we are still trying, and will continue to do so in this and future lifetimes.

Are people who think they are elves and faeries crazy?

The answer to that question is: sometimes. The normal world will drive nearly anyone crazy. You just need to look around you to see that at least a third of the general population are out of touch with reality in a serious way and a vast majority believe all sorts of ridiculous things about their particular god and the devil and how the world functions and other religious and superstitious mumbo jumbo without the least bit of scientific evidence and in fact against most of what we know to be essentially true about the nature of the world and the Universe.

So it is only to be expected that some of our kindred that come to us are crazy. They, after all, are fleeing an insane world and were sometimes reared by loony people. But the nature of Elfin is such that it is inclined in time to help one heal and particularly to heal one's emotional, mental and psychological selves and this has a very positive affect upon one's physical body as well.

On the other hand, if you ask do most of the people in the world think we are crazy for believing we are elves and fae folk, then, yes, they do. They even have an old expression for this, which is that one is "away with the faeries," meaning we are essentially out of it and nuts but often in a harmless fashion. And really, many of us have supported this notion and played upon it, for it allows us a certain amount of latitude in their world. They expect less of us and there is less pressure for us to conform to their petty customs and social "niceties," which are just meaningless to us.

On the other hand, if you ask would professional psychiatrists or psychologists see us as suffering from some disorder, that depends both upon the maturity of the therapist and of the elfae. As we said, some of us are crazy. How could we not be living among these insane normal folk? But believing one's to be an elf, or really from our point of view, living our lives as elves and thus magically and de facto being elves, is not a crazy thing to do. And every competent psychological professional (and we've known quite a few, some of them are our very good friends) would agree.

As we explained in the previous section, it is common for some folks to mistakenly think that we might suffer from Schizotypal Disorder since we do talk to trees and spirits and other things and listen to them as well. But if we truly suffered from that disorder, and nearly any other psychological disorder, it would make us essentially dysfunctional in the world and unable to navigate its treacherous waters. And while the world is not an easy place for most people to function within, and here we mean elfae and normal folk, we elfae generally do okay and are surely much more sane than many of the folks we encounter on a day to day basis, who are ranting half the time. Just out and out barking mad.

So, no we are not crazy for believing, thinking or, more importantly, being elves or faeries or pixies or whatever. Rather developed, mature and evolved elfin have a tendency to soothe and heal those around us and at the very least bring a bit of humor, light and creativity into their lives. And if we are crazy, well, we're certainly not crazy in a dangerous way as a lot of those folks are and that, in itself, speaks greatly in our favor.

Is there one term for elves, faeries and otherkin?

Otherkin surely is the most inclusive of terms for everything other, including elves, faerie folk in myriad types, pixies, brownies, vampires, Therians and Weres or various sorts and nearly everything else that isn't quite human or is, perhaps humanoid but not totally human, or maybe even human plus. This point is, we're not quite normal and are very glad that this is the case. Those who aren't normal and wish to be are rather sad creatures usually. This is the common compliant of those who are highly sensitive and psychics who wish that they didn't see or hear the things they did. They look upon their gifts as a curse and "just want to be normal." In time, of course, they will become normal. This may take lifetimes but eventually they will merge seamlessly among normal humanity, losing or letting go of the gifts that they didn't really want in the first place.

While those of us who aren't quite normal, or are in fact quite weird, and are glad of this fact, particularly when we look about us and see what normal humans are like and their tendency to kill and pollute everything including each other, will become increasingly eccentric and will be quite happy about it all (see our book *Living the Personal Myth: Making the Magic of Faerie Real in One's Own Life*).

But to return to our main theme, we created the word 'Elfae' when writing on elven listservs in the 90s and we still use this term today to refer to the Elfin and Faerie folk in general, which is to say elves, pixies, faeries, brownies and so on. But this doesn't tend to include vampires except as they are a manifestation of the Unseelie Elven, nor does it tend to cover Therians, except in the sense that often elfin wizards and shamans have shape shifting abilities or animal totems and familiars through whose bodies they can travel or use their eyes to view the world. But the difference is often one of control. Many Therians and Weres according to legend and lore have no control over when the change occurs, whereas elfin shamans ever do.

Fae, as a word, is also rather inclusive of all elfin faerie folk, for we are all really of Faerie and countenanced in its imagination, its growth and its flourishing. We are all Eldritch folk, born of the Wyrd (weird), radiant with the magic (except when we intentionally hide it to slip among those who are hostile to magic or go insane at the mere mention of it, either in fear of it or denial) and ever bringing starlight into a world that has blinded itself with its own false lights and pretended wonder. Whatever you choose to call yours'elf or us overall, Beloved, Otherkin, Elfae, or Fae, we wish you ever blessed in the light of Elfin and to go with a star upon your brow.

Elfin, Faerie or Elfland?

Through the course of time we have come to refer to the realms that we abide in as Elfin. We used to call it Elfland, like many writers, and we sometimes referred to it as Faerie but we have come to see these as terms that, at least in our minds, have a certain difference to them and thus, when we use them, we use them to delineate slightly different things. These are essentially our own definitions and we don't expect that others will necessarily agree with them but for those who are interested in what we are saying and what we mean in using these terms, here is an explanation of our terminology.

To us, Elfland always refers to a specific place, like England, France and Japan. But for the most part no such place seems to exist upon the Earth at the moment, although there are surely those who would like to create such a realm. There are those who would posit the idea that Elfland exists, in the sense that Faerie does, as a parallel realm that is connected to the Earth at certain places, particularly the wild places of Nature and we can surely see that. But as soon as you put forth that idea you begin to move away from Elfland as a specific place on Earth toward the idea of Elfin, which is a state of being, a people, a culture and a vibration that follows those peoples wherever we may be.

Thus when we speak of Elfin we are referring to the vibrational realm of our mutual elven existence. It follows us around, so to speak, and is born of our being and our interaction. The more of us there are who are living our lives as the elves we know ours'elves to be in harmony with each other, the more powerful this energy, vibration, state of being is.

When we abide in any particular place for an extended time, Elfin manifests Elfland. We make a connection to the land and the land begins to reflect our energy and vibration as we adapt to the weather and atmosphere of the land. If we lived in a particular place for more than a hundred years, then we might begin to think of that place as Elfland, but these elves, at least, are inclined to be a very migratory people ever moving and traveling from here to there. But then we are somewhat nomadic elves.

In a very real sense, the British Isles, which were once referred to as Albion, are Elfland, or certainly were. Alb comes from the root word for elf, elves, etc. Albion is the Land of the Elf Queen, or Elf Goddess, or Elfin Peoples. But peoples change, as do places. This is not to say that elves don't still live in Ablion, now called England, but we can hardly consider England to be Elfland anymore, although much of our ancient culture still abides there. After all, England produced Tolkien.

Yet, many of us have moved on and we have taken our Elfin with us. While we surely love the land, we are not attached to it in the same way that the legends of Dracula have him having to drag his native dirt around with him. We are more resilient than that and make compact with every land we live in or travel through, bringing introductory gifts for the genii loci, the regional spirits of the land.

Faerie, to our minds and as we have previously explained in this chapter, is vaster than Elfin and much wilder as well. There are all sorts of beings in Faerie. Surely many of the unseelie folk abide there. There are goblins and grimlens and orcs and all manner of folk who couldn't, until they find some semblance of enlightenment, enter into Elfin. Faerie is wild nature untamed and, at times, quite dangerous, whereas, Elfin is our Secret Magical Garden. We still let some wildflowers grow and certainly an Elven garden doesn't tend to be overly organized, but still, it is a safe place where none will come to harm unless they bring that harm upon thems'elves and none can enter in until they are mature enough as soulful spirits to do so.

This is not to say that we elves don't ever venture into Faerie. After all, we have come into this insane world on a mission to awaken our peoples, so from time to time we delve into the dreamlike realms of Faerie as well, where one may have quite pleasant dreams but may also encounter nightmares. The truth is most faeries prefer abiding in Elfin more than they do in Faerie proper, because they are safer there. But then, some of them have their wild side as well and there are times when they are determined to take a walk on the wild side, and that is surely true of most of us.

What's the difference between elves and faeries?

While both elves and fairies are fae, we are different tribes, actually a variety of different tribes as there are different tribes of both elves and of fairies. And this is not even counting the varieties of pixies, brownies and other related kindred. And we are a diversifying people as well, which means that as we evolve into the future, more and more types and tribes of elves and faeries will emerge.

This is similar to the Celtic peoples, who came after us, who were also not one people, but a vast variety of tribes that shared a common culture. The word Keltoi, itself, comes from the Greeks and was not the name those various peoples called themselves but a name given to them by outsiders. And it should be noted that while they shared a culture, they did not all speak the same language. Interestingly, and germane to our topic, Tolkien's elves also spoke different languages and variations on those languages. In the modern world, of course, elves and faeries, for the most part, are raised within the framework of other 'normal' cultures and thus speak the language of their upbringing and sometimes the lingua franca of our times.

We could say, tongue in cheek, the difference between elves and faeries is that "Fairies Fly and Elves Levitate." Since faerie folk tend to love to wear faerie wings as a symbol of their culture and we elves depend upon our spirits to uplift us. Our own tendency, of course, is not to love faerie wings so much as pointed ears. But then saying, "Fairies fly and Elves listen pointedly" just isn't as clever, is it?

We have observed that modern faeries, those in human bodies, are often more easily accepted in the world than most of we elven brothers and sisters. Fairies, even though they are considered by others to be "airy" or "flighty" (there is even a term in academic circles of being "airy fairy"), are often really adept in business matters and this enables them to move with greater facility in the world than we elves do. As it is, we elves are frequently more outcast and do not fit as smoothly into the world. And usually we elves do not care to merge into the world if we have to change ours'elves to do it. We prefer the freedom to express ours'elves more than we hunger for acceptance or financial success.

Of course, one might have both elven and faerie within hir, as we are a varied people and combinations of fae being and spirit are more common than not. There are surely those who like to flaunt their pure elven blood, but the reality of the elfin is that we are seldom actually snobbish, tend to be sensually inclined and find all manner of folk beautiful and thus intermingling with others is more likely to occur than not among the elfin. Although, this is probably true of the faerie folk as well and in that way we are rather alike. Some might say we are easy, but it would be more true to say we are easy when we wish to be.

It is important to understand that while the faerie folk make quite a show of being flighty and unreliable at times, this is mostly just a pose. This is a glamour they use to move through the world and they can be just as intent and dedicated to their designs as the elven. While we elven often seem aloof and snobbish, even arrogant to outsiders, we are really quite warm hearted most of the time, simply, for the most part, a little more inclined toward introversion than the often extroverted faeries, but this is just a generalization and the real difference between elves and faeries is even to be found in the difference between an individual elf and an individual faerie. Generalizations are a convenience but they seldom encompass the whole truth and quite often obscure it. And we elves ever strive to differentiate our preconceptions from reality and to judge each individual as an individual, and in our experience individuals always surprise us.

☙

Who are the half elves?

Many novels speak of half elves and surely this comes from the idea of races as they are typically defined in the world today as being an aspect of physical manifestation with certain physical features, such as skin color, type of hair, shape of nose or lips, etc. Tolkien called Elrond, we believe, half elven.

And surely if elves were a totally distinct physical type we could see the point in this, although not much of a point. However, we elves, particularly we Silver Elves, see race not so much as an aspect of physical characteristics but an aspect of character itself. It is a spiritual point of view rather than a material point of view. And in that sense, if we considered the Shining Ones to be purely elven, all of us who have yet to fully manifest ours'elves as elves are half elven or part elven, compared to them. We are in the process of becoming ever more elven by living our lives as elves.

The simple fact is that while there are certain tendencies for elves considering physicality, there are no exact features that define elves. We tend to be thin, but not always. Really, we are inclined to be the right weight for the body type we've chosen to inhabit. We often look younger than our age would indicate but that is comparing ours'elves to the normal folk who so often abuse their bodies and wear them out. However, the many trials that an elf can face in this life, the challenges and sometimes tragedies that one endures can affect this. And looking at race the way men define it, which is primarily skin color, we can be of any race or people whatsoever.

This is due to the fact that we are not only the Eldar/Elder race that is behind and at the root of all peoples, but because we have through time mixed with them both willingly, because, let's face it, elves are often easy going in temperament, and because the more dominant peoples have forced themselves upon us. Also, because we are a spiritual folk many of us have developed the ability between incarnations to choose what body we wish to be born in, dropping into this or that physical race or group of people as need and quest or even serendipity directs us.

For those who believe in the physical and genetic heritage of the elven, as we've descended from the Annunaki and the Scythians and other related tribes, the fact still holds true that we have merged with other peoples both willingly and unwillingly through the ages. This would seem to indicate that we are all in a sense half elven. Although Nicholas De Vere claimed he and a few others were of the pure elven bloodline, and this may be so. But genetics, because of the tendency to have dominant (dominating) and subdominant (otherkind) genes and tendencies, tells as that if two people offer their subdominant genes in the process of creation, we often get a relatively pure subdominant (elfin or other) type of being. We are all mutants in a sense anyway. At least, that's how most of us view ours'elves.

In the long run, however, as we said previously, we elves are not so concerned with what genetic lineage we may have appeared to be derived from, because it is our elven nature and character that really illuminates our being. Ultimately, it is our own actions, our own magic that defines us. We are elves because we wish to be elves, because we have chosen to be elves, because our magic has made us elves.

And in that sense, there are no half elves at all. We are all becoming more truly ours'elves but all perfect in potential in our inner being. While we may seem less than perfect in our manifestation in the world, more elven one day and less so the next, in the Elfin Realms we are completely and totally elven, although, we may be part pixie, or brownie or fae, as these elves are or some other combination. Our daughter always told us that she was a faerie elf and so she was.

In Elfin, you become what you truly wish to be and what you put energy/magic toward being. No one is a half elf, or part elf, unless they wish to be. We know that this concept is hard for some folks to absorb, having become used to viewing the world from a materialistic point of view, which is to be expected in this Kala Yuga, the most material of ages, but in time all elves come to understand that we are granters of wishes and the first wish we ever granted was our own wish to be elves.

༄

Are there really diminutive Fae Folk?

As we've said elsewhere and as explained in Nicholas De Vere's book *The Dragon Legacy*, the original elves and fae folk were conceived of as being more along the line of Tolkien's elves rather than the diminutive faerie folk, the little people with wings, that are so popular today. This is true, of course, because our ancestors where real people who lived in the world and although for the most part people tended to be shorter in those days they were still full sized human or humanoid beings of their age and time.

According to De Vere, the diminution of the fae folk into cute little flower fairies was a deliberate conspiracy to diminish the influence of the fae upon the normal world, to erase our memory from the peoples of the western world and to move those peoples away from the Fairy Faith to being more devotedly Christian. These elves, for our part, are not entirely certain that this is so. It is surely true that the Christians persecuted witches and Pagans and even alternate Christian faiths and coopted as much of the various Pagan beliefs and holidays as possible. However, making us seem like very little folk we think is less an effect of their designs than our own, and we feel it was more of an intentional act of our own camouflage to protect ourselves by seeming small and harmless rather than frightening humans.

And surely, making the fae cute little fairies did not erase the popular memory of us but increased it. People love the flower fairies and other little fae. We know we do love them, and our children did and do and loads of others do as well. For ages, we elfae have had to hide our culture in fairy tales, fiction and elf lore to preserve it and this, to us, was just another means of doing that.

So then, do those little fairies actually exist? Of course they do. For our own part, we have always recognized the butterflies, the dragonflies and the moths, the bees and lightning bugs as being faerie folk. The wasps and hornets and mosquitos, we expect, are Unseelie Folk. They have lives and consciousness of their own and these elves don't feel a need to anthropomorphize everything, giving them little human bodies as some folks seem determined to do. We can communicate with them as they are and we recognize them as fae peoples.

When we were very young we had a next door neighbor who decided to paint his house but when he got around to the side he found a bee hive in a corner junction. The bees were not all that happy that he was there and started buzzing around him. But he told them that if they would leave him alone to do his painting, he'd leave their hive alone as well. And they did and he did.

Still the notion that there are wee fairies that have human bodies has metaphysical significance to it in two primary ways. First, from an elven point of view we have all, including the Shining Ones, evolved through the various stages of manifestation from minerals to flora to fauna, etc. so will these faerie folk of moth, butterfly, dragonfly manifestation, evolve into some sort of humanoid form in the future. Just as we will eventually evolve into Shining Ones, who for their part will evolve into even higher and more subtle realms of being.

At the same time, while the idea of little fairy folk, miniature humans with wings, didn't seem to exist until a century or so ago, that doesn't mean that such beings don't now and haven't in the past existed on other dimensions. In fact, it should be clear that they do. And in loving them so much and visualizing them regularly, as many do, particularly children, that we are drawing them into this realm and dimension and giving them energy that they can use to manifest here, which is why there are those who have had sightings and relationships with these beings.

As time goes on, if this popular fervor for these beings continues, they will be able to cross over from their dimension ever more fully and manifest here in complete material form, which is to say everyone will be able to see them. Our love and interest is attracting them here and enabling them to more fully manifest. Of course, it will probably be aeons before they are completely substantial here for continuing periods of time, instead just dropping in now and again. But in the meantime, dear kindred, we have each other and Elfin to create and manifest upon the Earth, which is why we are here in the first place. Yes?

ᘍ

Are elves related to angels?

What most folks would call angels, these elves call the Shining Ones. The Shining Ones are our elven ancestors who have evolved through time, advanced in their magic, and matured in their spiritual development and have progressed to more powerful and more subtle dimensions of being, where they are not only closer to the heart of Elfin but are in realms where their thoughts and intentions are more quickly realized and manifested and thus they are more magically powerful. They do not need, in the way that we do, the buffer that exists between our thoughts and magical realization. Their thoughts are clearer, more focused and much less inclined toward the inner conflict and debate that many of us in these more material seeming realms encounter. And the fulfillment of their wishes can be nearly instantaneous, whereas ours may take a while, but that is generally for our own good until we have more precise control over our own wills and thoughts. The Shining Ones are more on the line of Tolkien's conception of elves in their most advanced stages than most of we elven currently manifesting upon the Earth are as yet able to be.

Unlike the concept of angels, who are created 'as is' by their god and are ever unchanging, unless they fail to obey and therefore go 'bad', the Shining Ones were once rather like us. Once children, so to speak, and we, for our own part, will eventually evolve to the point of being much like they are now. Of course, by that point, it is quite possible that they will have evolved even further and will be deeper or closer to the source that is the Divine Magic from which all things arise and which connects all that is. Thus the Divine Magic may be defined, quite rightly, as love. Which is why, to the elves, love and magic are seen as being nearly synonymous.

Elves don't, for the most part, have the idea, which so many egocentric individuals have, that the Shining Ones are our personal Guardian Angels. Which is to say, we don't believe there is one angel/Shining One who is assigned to follow us around our entire lives and guide us. There are Shining Ones who are related to us and by that we mean really related in this sense that they are our relatives, our ancestors, cousins and siblings, in a manner of speaking, and so forth and they do look out for us, as say our parents may look out for us when we are very young. But the more evolved we become, the older we get in a sense, the less they need to watch over us and the more responsibility we assume for our own lives and evolution.

And as we proceed even further, we assume responsibility not only for our s'elves but for our others as well and in doing that we truly begin to step into the realms of the Shining Ones and become as they are. This is the way to Elfin evolution. The way to the evolution of our s'elves as individual soulful spirits and the way by which elves may attain the true royalty of our heritage. Would you be a Shining One? Take care of your others. Would you be an Elf Lord or Lady, Elfin Prince or Princess, Elvish King or Queen, look after all of your kindred, nurture, support and empower them. Would you be a great spirit? A great soul? An Elfae wizard, druid, wise one? Do all that you can to foster our kindred, each and everyone, and the elfae nature in everyone and live your life in such a way as to be an example of true elfinness on each and every day. This is the Elven Way. This is the path into the realms of the Angelic Shining Ones.

"We are not born elfin but Elfin born, which means it is not our bodies that make us elven folk, but our inner spirits."

—*Wisdom of the Eldars*

Chapter 2:
Elven Magic

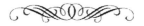

> Because elves love magic and it is an integral part of being elven, it is important to understand our magic. Our magic is the magic of enchantment and healing. We get many questions from people about elven magic, what kind we do and if we have special elven magical traditions and rituals. Here in this chapter, you will find are our responses to some of these questions.
>
> "Magic is Love is Magic!"

What is Elven Magic?

Magic is generally defined as the application of ones will to create various effects or achieve ones intentions. And surely Elven Magic would adhere to this definition as well. However, Elven Magic traditionally, both in reality and fiction, Fairy Tales and Faerie Lore, has associated the elves with the form of magic called Enchantment (see our book *The Keys to Elfin Enchantment* for more on this most elven art).

Enchantment seeks to fulfill its will especially through the enchanting or charming of the Universe and the individuals we desire to influence. It is not so much about compelling them to submit to our will but rather charming them into willingly fulfilling our desired intentions because they find us intriguing and wondrous and feel themselves benefited and fulfilled in aiding us and giving us what we desire. They seek to please us because we have inspired and pleased them, filled them with joy and helped bring meaning and purpose into their lives.

Thus elven enchantment depends a great deal upon the maturity and development of the individual's spirit, soul and personality. Most forms of magic, while certainly being benefited by having a mature magician performing the art, don't actually require the magician to have a good spirit, a decent soul and especially not a pleasing personality. A strong spirit is certainly a great help but no soulfulness or very little is required from most magicians and they can have, as fiction informs us and as history attests, the most noxious, nefarious or downright cantankerous personalities. Elves, however, to truly develop our powers of enchantment need to awaken the divine within ours'elves for there is nothing more attractive to man, beast or spirit than the ecstatic nature of the Divine Magic.

ತ

What is rainbow magic that the Silver Elves often speak about?

According to a Hopi Prophecy the Rainbow People will come and save the peoples of the Earth. The Earth, itself, according to the elves, doesn't need saving. It is humanity and the other creatures upon it that are truly in danger from man unkinds' and others' predations. The Earth will do quite well without humanity. But we elves and fae folk would rather not have it that way. We'd much rather harmonize with Nature and find/create a place where all peoples, human and otherwise, may be successful and flourish.

Thus, rainbow magic is really the magic of the rainbow people, which is to say all the Elfae (elven faerie folk) and others that work together to create a better situation for all of us—a true elven civilization upon the Earth. A place where everyone is free to express hir own s'elf and hir own nature as long as they don't interfere with others. This idea of the Rainbow People, the combined elven and fae folk along with all others, is essentially an Aquarian notion and befits the Aquarian Age that is still in the process of birthing. It is, as we've said elsewhere, the essential idea that we can all do our own thing together. It puts forth the notion that win-win situations are not only possible but preferable and that we are able not only to agree to disagree but we can also agree to let each other, as much as possible, pursue our own interests and development. There is room in Elfin for all sincere and willing folk that chose to be there.

These may seem in some ways like new ideas (some folks might even fluff them off as New Age, a term that is held in scorn by numerous folks, although these elves have never been precisely clear about why they do so, nor has anyone been able to tell us) but like the Hopi Prophecy and the notion of the Aquarian Age, these are actually something that have been handed down to us from the Ancestors. They foresaw our coming and rejoiced in the fact that it was so, as we rejoice and take heart in those who are yet to come.

Another way to look at this, however, is in the Seven Rays of Manifestation, which are each accorded a color associated with the Rainbow. The three primary colors being the first three rays and the blending of those colors (the secondary colors) being the last three rays and the fourth, by its nature, being a place of synthesis. For our own part we see the fourth ray as being of the tonal scale, thus white to black with all the grays in between, and thus also silver. We elves particularly associate with this ray, although any individual elf may have another ray as hir dominant propensity.

But this brings us back to the Rainbow Magic and the fact that there is a blending occurring. Elves, while we tend to be, first and foremost, enchanters, are also wizards, witches, sorcerers, magicians, conjurors and healers, herbalists, shamans, and every other sort of magician that uses hir magic to manifest Elfin in a bright and positive way that is fulfilling and healing for all involved. This is the Rainbow Magic, uniting our powers to create something truly wondrous for everyone, a world of shining radiance where love rules, magic illuminates, and we dance together in joy forever in a world brilliant with color.

Do elves do ceremonial magick?

Well, we have. We've done and experimented with every form of sane magic that we've come across. Our *The Book of Elven Magick 1 &2* suggest possibilities for doing ceremonial and ritual magic. But as is so often the case with these elves, we are only making suggestions in order to inspire our kindred to create their own rituals and ceremonies if that is their desire.

For our own part, we don't really have any ceremonies that we perform. If called to do so we, of course, could whip one up at a moment's notice, and we are certainly not against ceremony, we just don't really have that many formal occasions to celebrate or mark with ceremony.

We have done magick in a magic circle, if you wish to call that ceremonial magick and we have evoked spirits into a magical triangle and we have observed the traditional rules concerning this art as we did so. Still most of what we did was still improvised on the spot. There is very little ritual or repetition in our magic circles or ceremonies. We are a very impromptu folk.

But we have also attended ceremonies that various pagan friends have conducted, as well as having attended Christian and other ceremonies. These include graduation ceremonies that we took part in, weddings, baptisms, etc. (In fact, years ago on a journey, a sort of Faerie Rade through Arizona, a young man that we encountered there asked Zardoa if he would baptize him and so Zardoa put together an impromptu baptism for him. We are rather all purpose elves.)

Yet, at the same time, while the magic we do tends to be ad hoc and on the fly most of the time, we can see the value in having ceremonies that have been rehearsed and include rituals. While we have experience in improvisational theatre, we wouldn't much care for it if every movie we watched was unrehearsed and improvised. We can see the importance and power in a certain amount of preparation and if we were dealing with a large crowd/audience we'd probably rehearse our performance in order to give it the most impact and dramatic flair. But since these elves are generally doing magic

Zardoa Silverstar gives Elven Blessings, an elven magical healing ritual.

unseen in the world, the only thing that really matters is that we do it as sincerely and effectively as we are able.

~

Do elves do ritual magic?

First, let us say that many people use the terms ceremonial magick and ritual magick as interchangeable and we don't object to them doing so, we have probably done so our own s'elves. But if we wish to be a bit technical about it, ceremonial magick probably has more to do with a ceremony, which is to say marking a special event or occasion, as say the ceremony when a king or queen is crowned or a president sworn in, or even a graduation ceremony.

Ritual, on the other hand, bears the idea of something that is repeated and probably on a regular basis, almost a habit. In that way the Catholic mass may sometimes be called a ceremony, because it is celebrating the miraculous life and death and rebirth of Christ, but really is in most cases a ritual that is repeated on a weekly basis at the very least. This is not to say that the Catholic Church doesn't have ceremonies, as for instance when a new pope is installed, or a priest raised up to be a bishop or cardinal, or a nun or a priest takes their vows. But the every Sunday mass really is more in the form of a ritual than a ceremony. But it is easy to see how these two terms have become somewhat interchangeable.

We elves probably do more ritual magick than ceremonial magick but in saying that it might be important to point out that when we say we do ritual magic we don't necessarily mean we are evoking spirits in a magic circle. Our ritual magick is not usually combined with ceremony in a uniform fashion, for as we previously explained our ceremonies are more impromptu and follow little traditions like the ones you may have already experienced in many Pagan ceremonies. For instance, we surely may call the spirits in a magic circle, but not as a ritual in the same way calling the same spirits from the same directions year after year for a particular ceremony. We would be more likely to consult the elven oracles (perhaps using *The Elfin Book of Spirits* or *The Elements of Elven Magic*) to find the spirits that need to join us for that particular day and magical occasion.

Rather than rituals in ceremonies, we have certain daily rituals we tend to do, like having tea and toast or home baked gingerbread for breakfast each day, or doing the dishes, and in doing these rituals we often turn them into a bit of magic. And, frankly when we say we have breakfast each day, it is good to understand that we generally get up somewhere between 10:30 a.m. and Noon, and have 'breakfast' at around 1:30 p.m. to 2 p.m. We're not sure that still counts as breakfast in some people's minds, but it is when we usually break our fast. And we have other little magics we do most days, (this routine being altered at times when we are off adventuring), sending blessings out into the world to our kindred and doing what we can to help, heal and awaken our kin. These are also little bits of ritual magic, but very informally done, simply somewhat repetitive in nature, although open to change and modification at any time we think of some way to do what we are doing better and more effectively. We also often enjoy painting our magical sigils on rocks and leaving them during our travels in various places around the world, during which we give our elven blessings. Both the artistic creative process of making the rocks and the elven blessings we give while placing them are an elven ritual for us and something we love to do over and over, yet each time it is quite different for each location requires a different healing energy.

So, yes, these elves do ritual magic, but with the same formality that we do the dishes (which is to say, often but quite informally and as efficiently as possible) and the same attention to detail and love that we give to preparing our meals.

※

What is the difference between "Magical Thinking" and superstition?

Jean Piaget in outlining his cognitive development stages for children spoke of a stage that is distinguished by the child's tendency toward Magical Thinking. What he and other psychologists mean by magical thinking we would call superstitious thinking, although there is a certain similarity between the two. In their definition of Magical Thinking, there is a false connection in the mind of the individual, particularly a child, in causal relationships, which is to say effects and what caused them to happen.

For instance, we once had an elfin woman who lived with us for a while, and one day she saw Zardoa using one of the slim wooden sticks he uses for doing the I Ching to get some wax out of his ear. We know, you're probably disgusted, but it was the best tool available for the job at the time. This elf woman went nearly crazy when she saw him doing this and it wasn't because he was getting ear wax on the end of a Ching stick, or that he might puncture his ear drum, as you might expect from some parent warning a child about putting relatively sharp objects in hir ear. When Zardoa asked her what the problem was she said that she had had a friend who used to do the same thing and she had died of cancer, as though using thin sticks of wood to clean one's ear somehow caused cancer.

Now that is essentially what Piaget and other psychologists and anthropologists mean by Magical Thinking, although we'd call that superstitious thinking. As it applies to children, they would say that when a child is angry with hir parent and says, "I hate you," with the full force of childhoods emotional energy and then the parent has an accident, such as an automobile accident, the child may think that sHe caused the accident, falsely attributing hir hate to the effect of the accident.

However, from a magical point of view, these two events are not necessarily unconnected. The psychic force of the child's anger can and does have effects upon the world. If your boss cusses you out and then you are so upset that you have an accident on the way home, these are not unconnected events. They are not scientifically connected events between cause and effect, which is to say magic is not like chemistry in the sense that if you put together the right ingredients in the correct proportions in a specific sequence, a predictable result will always, or nearly always, occur. Every time a child is angry at hir parent the parent doesn't have an accident. But that doesn't mean that such actions, such magic doesn't have effects, just that they are not replicable by empirical science.

And magic generally is thought of as having less direct effects. We can surely understand that if someone is upset by an argument, as for instance in the example of one's boss yelling at one, that one might be effected by this and an accident occur. But in "Magic" Thinking, we go a step further. We believe that the mere psychic atmosphere can affect an outcome. Thus one's boss, or spouse or friend doesn't have to yell at you directly. They can even be angry at you without you knowing of it, but that anger has effects in the world and if they direct it at you intentionally, it can have an effect upon you, causing you to have an accident. Magical Thinking is not superstitious thinking. It is not saying there is a connection where there cannot possibly be one. It merely sees a wider range of interconnectedness.

In that sense magic is a bit more like medicine than chemistry. If a doctor gives a person a certain medicine, it is expected to help them heal, but sometimes because of the unique and individual nature of our bodies, it doesn't and occasionally it makes things worse. This is, in part, why ancient Asian medicine emphasized medicines that were designed for the specific needs of a particular individual.

At the same time, while the feelings of a child can be very powerful and focused in their anger, they lack the conscious direction of more mature magic. And surely there must be some general binding on the magic of children otherwise nearly every parent in the world would have died or had a terrible accident. We might point out that while a child might be angry with hir parent, most don't really want them to die. Their own needs and desires are a restraint on the effect of their anger.

It has been suggested that the hormonal imbalance that happens when the child becomes a teenager is sometimes the cause of poltergeists, but again this is undirected magic, unintentional magic that flings things about and makes a mess.

But, it is still magic. It is just not quite Magical Thinking, however, so much as Magical Feeling.

As we mature and become more logical (usually or hopefully) in our understanding of the world and its connections and the link between cause and effect, most people tend, however, to lose that Magical Feeling that was so very powerful, if somewhat erratic, and our magic becomes conscious and ritual or spell oriented, but often lacking in the power and imagination that gave it so much juice in the first place. This is, of course, why shamans chant and drum to create the ecstatic state, that inner feeling of meditative, focused and potent joy to empower their will as well as enchant the spirits.

When we bring those two things together, Magical Thinking and Magical Feeling, our enchantments become far more powerful. But still magic is not like empirical science. There are greater forces at work quite often than our own small desires. That doesn't mean that our magic won't work, but it is wise to understand that we live in a wider world and that the Shining Ones watch over us as we do our children and always seek the best for us. Our magic isn't always quick or automatic, but it eventually fulfills our true will which is to be our true s'elves. And this is not just Magical Thinking, nor is it superstition but an understanding of the true nature of the Universe, which is magical to its very core.

"If magic were money the elves would be the richest folks in the world, instead we are usually the luckiest."

—Old Elven Saying

Do elves curse people?

We've said before but we will say it again, these elves usually only curse people when we are driving on the highway, and that doesn't really count. Well, not much. It doesn't have true intention behind it. It is just letting off steam and doesn't bear the full force of magic behind it, although it is still an emotive expression and we have to face the fact that such powers going out into the world do have an effect even if that effect isn't as powerful as it might be if that emotion had the full weight of our intention behind it.

Generally speaking, however, we don't put curses on people because first of all we are elves and our principle magic is enchantment. Curses are not that enchanting, really. They don't make us more attractive to people. They could make people afraid of us, but for the most part, except under extreme conditions, we don't really wish that.

Recently, we've seen something going around the internet saying the problem with witches today is that nobody fears us anymore (for we are also Elven Witches), implying that we would be better off if people had a healthy and fearful respect of us. This is rather like the idea that we sometimes encounter in movies and television shows when a person says they'd rather be feared than loved. We elves, for our part, would much rather be loved and do our upmost, most of the time, to not put the fear of the elves into people, which is to say the fear of the supernatural and the unknown into them.

We've often found that when we have visitors or guests who are not elven or not witches, magicians, etc. that if we happen to leave them alone for awhile in what we sometimes refer to as our elven library and museum, these folks will let their imaginations run away with them and wind up scaring themselves silly. We, of course, assure them there is nothing to be afraid of because we elves tend to bless people, not curse them, and there is no malignant magic flowing around our Eald.

And this is the truth. For the most part, we elves don't curse people, although we could, rather we tend to bless them, even when they have done ill to us. And there is a good reason for us doing so and it is not that we have forgiven them, although we surely will if they make amends, but because we have found that blessings are far more efficacious than curses.

If we curse someone, they will naturally resist it. However, if we bless someone they will usually let that blessing in and if they don't, and some do resist blessings, they lose out on that magic. Simultaneously, all magic eventually returns to the sender multiplied manifold and thus what returns to us are blessings. If they reject them, they return sooner, but if they accept them, they return more powerfully.

Part of the reason we bless people who "cross" us, is that we don't wish for them to become worse, which is to say to become even more abhorrent because we cursed them, but to heal and become better people. At the same time, it is a simple fact of magic that when we elves bless someone they have to clear up their karma to receive that blessing and thus become a better person, therefore in blessing them we have indirectly caused them to draw their own karma down on themselves. This is an elvish trick, of course, but it works wonderfully.

This is similar to the fact that when people are rude to us we are most often very courteous and polite in return not only because we are elves and are just polite by nature and love courtesy, but because our kindness in response to them is so totally not what they expected that they become discombobulated by our response and we love to see the confusion on their faces as they try to figure out what just happened. Often they just mutter something inane and wander off perplexed leaving us smiling and laughing quietly in their wake. We are mischievous elves. It must be the pixie in us. But we love to love everyone, even those who don't seem to deserve it or want it, because they need it even more.

❧

What do the Silver Elves think of Using Reiki in their Magic?

We elves, for the most part, particularly these elves, are interested in everything having to do with everything we are interested in. Since magic and healing are two disciplines of especial interest to these elves, it is only natural that we encountered Reiki as we went about our magical workings.

Curiously, this has come about almost entirely without us pursuing it in anyway. We have heard of Reiki and knew of other elves who practiced it, but we simply hadn't gotten around to actually exploring it ours'elves. Then, about thirty years ago, one of our sisters, whom we were visiting at the time, was in some of her early levels of Reiki Mastery and wanted to give us first level Reiki initiation. We agreed merely to be of service to her. It seemed important to her and we didn't really care one way or the other, so we acquiesced and she initiated us.

However, we didn't do anything with it or explore it any further at the time. But, ten years later, a friend of our son's came over one time and she was also developing into being a Reiki Master and wanted to initiate us. So again, we agreed, but also again, only because it was important to her in some way. In this case, she gave us first and second-degree initiations. And once again, we accepted it, but did nothing to pursue it any further.

Another ten years passed by and our elven sister, the one who had initiated us the first time, told us that while she had a third degree initiation and had become a Reiki Master, that she had let her practice slip over time and that she wanted us to become Reiki Masters so we could re-initiate her. Alas, this required that she first give us third degree initiation. So she sent us several books by Diane Stein on the subject that we studied to develop our own skills and when next we visited her, she gave us the third degree initiation and then we turned around and did the same for her.

This surely was a rather lengthy and roundabout way of learning this art, but in the end we became fascinated with Reiki and began using it in our own healing practice and now do so daily sending out energy to our kindred wherever they may be, blessing and awakening the elfin and all who are open to a better, more magical life.

Elven Blessings, dear Kin!

What is the Orb of Healing?

Years ago we came upon a greenish glass globe of the type that are sometimes used in connection with fishing nets by Asian sea fishermen. These elves are not fishers in that sense and had no use for the orb in that fashion. However, we really liked this orb and decided to keep it and use it in our magic and made it a part of our elven home.

We have several magic tables in our home. Most folks would call these altars, but since we don't worship any particular gods or goddesses and since these are areas where we store various of our magical implements and also where we charge various items for magic, we call them magic tables, although, sometimes they are really magic shelves or magic spaces. But then our whole apartment is a magic space, the realm that we call Eldafaryn, the mystical and magic aura of energy that surrounds our being and our magic. Our Eald, our little realm of Elfin.

At the center of one of these "magic tables," we have the Orb of Healing that we created from the glass ball that we had come upon about thirty years ago. We painted it with fluorescent paint so that it glows in the dark when the lights get turned out. As it happens, this particular magic table is in our bedroom, so every night the radiance of the Orb of Healing glows upon us as we fall asleep, soothing and healing us.

We instilled this orb with healing energy and, of course, use it when we feel we are getting sick, although "knock on wood," or "pat the trees," we've been very lucky thus far in our lives and have been graced with very good health. Still, occasionally we have need of the Orb's powers and we absorb its energy as needed.

However, mostly we use it for putting healing energy into various magical objects that may come our way: amulets, talismans and other items. We use it for clearing objects of past vibrations and attuning them to our own magic. And naturally thence these objects always have a bit of healing energy in them that they spread whenever we take them about or place them around our elven home.

Once every decade we repaint the Orb of Healing with new and more fluorescent paint. This was not a plan on our part; it just somehow turned out that way. In our minds, it not only renews the energy but also makes it stronger. Thus its powers are ever increasing and, in fact, the more it is used the stronger it gets.

We know that someday, when we have passed to another realm or perhaps simply by accident, it will be broken and when that happens all the healing energy that has been stored within it will be released into the wider world. While the world surely needs this energy, there is no hurry in our minds for this to happen. We know that however crazy things seem to be at times, and the longer it takes for this healing energy to be released, the more powerful the release will be. And surely, it will happen in its own time, when the time is right, and elfin healing shall penetrate into the world touching the lives of all our kindred for the better and soothing and healing the world as well.

"The fabric of Elfin is a cross weave of magic and imagination, which is why elves find inspiration everywhere."

—*Old Elven Saying*

Are all elves mystics?

Mysticism is the art of becoming one with the Absolute, or what we elves would refer to as the Magic or the Divine Magic. This state of mystical union with the Divine as it exists in any and all things is achieved through a state of ecstasy or an altered state of consciousness that takes on a spiritual or religious significance for the individual who attains this shamanic condition of union. It bears with it the idea that one might attain insight into ultimate or hidden, occult truths, magical truths, and a greater understanding of one's own evolution and the process of human development overall as well as the course of life for all Being.

From the point of view of outsiders, we elves, when we don't seem totally imaginary, are nearly all experienced as being mystic or mystical in some way. It is a curious fact that for those who are not of our kind, encountering us can be a sort of mystical experience. We evoke the supernatural in their minds as well as unleash the imaginal in their psyches. Alas, when this occurs they frequently scare themselves silly with all sorts of dire imaginings based upon spooky shows they've watched. But we usually do our best to soothe them and give them some secure anchor to reality.

Like all people, but even more so, we elves are a myriad folk and we approach life and the Universe and our relationship to Elfin and Faerie from a variety of different directions and ways of being. We are artists and scientists and doctors, lawyers, magicians and mystics and much else, however in our own way of being those things and not necessarily quite in the way that they are imagined, experienced or practiced in the normal world.

At the same time, we elven tend to be a Renaissance folk so we are seldom just one thing but pursue a variety of paths all at the same time. We are doctors and artists, scientists and mystics and many other things and combinations according to our own yearning to know, learn and develop as soulful elven spirits.

However, there is truth to the fact that we elves generally have a closer relationship with Nature and the magical aspects of the Universe than many other folk and that relationship and our understanding and awareness of that relationship is rather mystical in and of itself. And there is the fact that we often are inclined to be more in harmony with ours'elves and Nature than many others and this instills us with a sense of contentment and happiness that is surely akin to and at the doorstep of ecstasy. It is easy for us to step into the realms of the mystical because we are often quite close to them in our everyday life.

Still, not every elf, in fact quite few, will choose to spend a great deal of their time in near constant communion with the Divine Magic on such a deep and profound level in the fashion that monks and certain nuns may do. We each have our own quest, our mission, our dharma to fulfill chosen by our own nature and our own souls. Although, it is true that some of us also have a geas upon us, an aspect of Karma that compels us to accomplish this or that thing in order to advance in our evolutionary development. It is a burden in a sense but one we've chosen through our own actions to carry, and in bearing it we are bound to grow stronger and step closer to Elfin and our true nature in its accomplishment.

So, is every elf a mystic? Yes and no.

How do you give Elven Blessings?

If you have joined us on Facebook (and if you have not done so already then we certainly invite you to do so), then you may have noticed that we often promote our books online. We currently have 41 books available and while we don't directly sell them ours'elves, we do put them about so our kindred will know of their existence, if they don't already and, of course, to let those who haven't heard of us know of our existence as well. We are ever eager to connect with our kin and always on the look out for more of our kindred, for there is almost nothing more interesting, inspiring and exciting for us than encountering our true elf kin. Time spent with our kindred, even online, is very thrilling for us. The variety of elfae folk is ever amazing to us and we are constantly learning new things as we encounter new kin (or frequently old kin that we are meeting anew in this lifetime).

Often when we post these, not ads exactly but, notifications or signposts concerning our books, our kindred will click the "like" or "love" button and we endeavor to respond by sending them Elven Blessings of various sorts. This is not simply a matter of saying, "Elfin Blessings," to a particular person but truly sending them our blessings, in response to their support, from our hearts and minds through the psychic atmosphere of the world and more importantly through the ethers of Elfin that connects us all. All elfae are linked through the kindreth we share, the love we have of each other and of Elfin, and the Magical and Mystical ambience of Elfin, what we might call the Mists of Faerie, now and through the lifetimes.

There is intention behind the action of writing out, "Elvish Blessings," to someone and that combination of intention and action, as you well know, equals magic. We are not merely writing or saying, "Be Blest", but meaning it as well. Sending it forth with our love and our heartfelt desire that each may have a better life.

Of course, since elves are magical people by our very natures and some of us, as these elves, are students of the Magical Arts and have been for many lifetimes, we are well aware that magic always returns to the sender. The light of the sun shines forth but eventually the sun will burn itself out, collapse and the light it so generously gave out will begin to return to it. Thus in blessing others we are truly blessing ours'elves, just on a sort of time delay. It is rather like a savings account of magic. And since magic always returns three-fold, or really seven-fold for elves, there is quite a bit of interest accumulated as well.

Therefore we bless you beloved kindred, you who are reading these words, that you might be fulfilled and happy and successful in life and that all your true dreams will manifest into the reality of this world transforming your life for the better and sparking your evolution toward your true nature as you inwardly desire to be. And we know that you will find your way to Elfin where your kindred ever await you with open arms.

"Once one encounters Elfin, the experience lingers like one's first kiss."

—*Ancient Elven Enchantment Knowledge*

Chapter 3:
More About Who the Elves Are

> These are some of the specific questions that people have asked us about who elves are both spiritually and physically. You will find in reading this chapter that we can not really look at the physical characteristics of an elf without talking about the more important spiritual aspects of an elf. These questions are generally asked when people are trying to determine if they are an elf or some Otherkin and want to know some way to determine if they have the characteristics and spiritual makeup of an elf. You will find as you read that we feel that the Elven Way is through having the spirit of Elfin and that your physical makeup is not what defines you as an elf.

How can an elf be born from a man, pixie, etc.?

It is a curious fact that elves and elfae of various sorts, types and tribes are often raised by some quite normal folk, or at least folk who appear to be normal even though there is often something exceptional about them. By this we mean that they are quite willing to fit into normal society and commonly yield to peer pressure and are typically successful at appearing to be normal when in fact there is an aspect that is different about them that goes unregarded or is ignored for the most part by those around them.

It is also a fact that an elf might be born of pixies or vice versa or a brownie from a couple of goblins or whatever. This reinforces the idea that we Silver Elves commonly propose that elfae nature is more a matter of spirit and character than of genetics. Although, the reality that a different sort of being arises from a combination of other beings is not entirely unknown in the material world, even if it is a bit rare. But then rare is what we elves are all about.

You cannot get a cow from two horses, no matter how different the breeds of the horses may be. For you cannot breed between species. Thus a pig couldn't breed with a goat and produce something different or unique, although in long Ages past this was possible, in fact it was the rule, according to Elven Lore, which is how centaurs and satyrs and various other combinations of being came into manifestation. Thus a Palamino horse may come into being from the combination of two different breeds of horses, although it is not in fact a breed of its own. Donkeys or asses are bred with horses to create mules, for they are another form of the horse species. The evolutionary notion of mutation, of course, further supports the idea of something unique or different arising from a species as it adapts to various environments or as DNA itself decides to play around.

But there is also the reality of subdominant genes. Thus a red head may be born of two individuals who don't have red hair but carry the recessive gene for red hair. So, too, may elves be a recessive genetic type that come into being even though one's parents don't appear to be elven. Such recessive genes could be passed on for generations until they come together to produce what in the normal world would be seen as a pure elven type if, in fact, the normals recognized the existence of we elven at all.

Some elves may bristle at the idea that our elfae genetic strain is recessive, but the fact that we have receded and hidden from man and others for ages speaks to this idea at least metaphorically and the fact that we are not usually dominant people does so as well. We do not generally attempt to dominate situations or have power over others. We are noted for tending to hide from the world, use camouflage, mimicry and other means of protection, blending into Nature in all its guises fairly well, including making our way through the asphalt jungle that men like to create when necessary.

Still, for these elves the spiritual definition of the elven nature seems more logical to us. But then we elves have a wider view of the world and the Universe than many have and we have an experience with and understanding of parallel worlds and dimensions. While we are, in fact, rather fond of our physical bodies, we don't identity ours'elves based upon our bodies or body type. Nor do we define our kindred on that basis either. For us the only true way to know if someone is of the elfin is if they live their lives as elves. And to us, the only way to know if they are our kin or elf friends is if they are loving and friendly. We are elven magicians and enchanters. Titles mean very little to us. Action, which is to say magic, is nearly everything.

"No matter how humble our surroundings may be, in our hearts we elves always abide in Elfin."

—*Old Elven Saying*

Are there any real and absolute physical characteristics of being Elven?

No, not really. Pointed ears? Sometimes. We love them, but due to adaptation to fit into a hostile world of normal folks, we have often bred them out in order not to be killed for having pointed ears. Being thin? Usually. But most often we are just the appropriate weight for our body type, whatever it may be. And we'd like to point out that we once knew an elfin sister who went with a group of other elves to a farm and drank, along with them, fresh, unpasteurized milk. Alas, she got a parasite from doing so, which the others for some reason did not, and within a few months had gained nearly a hundred pounds. And no matter how little she ate, she continued to increase in weight until the doctors finally figured out what was going on.

So, should we have said this sister was no longer elven just because she, through no real fault of her own and not even due to a habit of her lifestyle, became overweight? How would that be fair? How would that even be elven to judge her so harshly? And what right do we have to judge other elves who are also struggling in their own way to cope with life?

Elvenness must be based upon something other than arbitrary physical characteristics. Being elven is and must ever be a matter of character rather than characteristic. Our bodies die and fade, changing from lifetime to lifetime, but our character endures and informs our being throughout incarnations to come. Our elven spirit being born again and again. That is what truly makes us elfin.

Is being an elf a matter of blood of genetic heritage?

There are those that proclaim that being an elf is only a matter of bloodline descent and while we agree that there are those who are descended from those people from which the tales of elves seem to originate, we simply cannot agree that elfinness is inherited. Our experience tells us that this is simply not the case. We see elfinness as being of the spirit and not requiring an inherited bloodline. Only the pursuit of the Elven Way, of living one's life as an elf, is a true indication of elfinness.

Even Nicholas de Vere who makes such claims in his books notes that everyone in the world, or most everyone, is likely to have at least a bit of elven blood in their veins. He contends, however, that his is purer and less undiluted and thus he has the right to consider hims'elf elven, while most others do not. Again, however, he offers us no DNA test results to back this up. While we respect his historical works, we have always taken issue with his exclusiveness when it comes to elfinness. Our belief is that if a person says they are an elf or Otherkin then we believe them. There is no bloodline requirement to be an elf as De Vere asserts, nor would bloodline assure that the person was an elf in spirit, which is the only requirement for being an elf.

Often those who make such claims as being of the elven bloodline present absolutely no evidence that it is so. They expect, like certain modern politicians, that we will accept their declarations without any data and often contrary to known facts. Some give us long genealogical charts but what they don't give us thus far is the evidence of a DNA test, demonstrating that their blood is as pure as they say it is.

Even if this were so, we'd still disagree with De Vere. If being elven and aspiring to elfin being were simply a matter of heritage then all one's ancestors would have made such a claim and pursued the path of the Elven and we see no evidence that this is so either.

And even if it were so, even if generation after generation in an individual's family had proclaimed they were elves, we'd still disagree because as elven beings, we are primarily beings of spirit, not of matter. We, through the lifetimes, gain the power to choose what sort of body we may wish to manifest in, from whatever bloodline we fancy based upon our own needs, goals or mission that we have to accomplish in any particular life form.

To us, the mere fact that one aspires toward being an elf is, in itself, an indication of one's essential elfinness. Who but an elf would wish to be an elf? And if all things derive from material being, as materialistic minded individuals believe, then why would we wish to be elves and live our lives as elves, if we were not genetically programmed to do so?

Even if we accept the idea that you are elves even though you don't have pointed ears, what about those folks who claim to be dragons, or werewolves or other mythical beings? It is true that those who claim to be dragons and certain other beings cannot be so in a physical sense, at least at this point, but just as we are elves because of the way we live, so are they dragons because of their inner spiritual longings and natures. This is not totally dissimilar to the fact that we call some men old goats or chickens or some such or that some folks derogatorily call certain women cows or old hens, or that we refer to certain men and women as dogs, although meaning different things in doing so. Besides the fact that these are often meant as insults, it is sometimes also an observation of the individual's character.

When individuals say that they are dragons, they don't mean, unless they are totally out of touch with reality, that they have the physical form of a dragon. They mean they spiritually and "imaginally" relate to being a dragon and in the world of the imaginal, a quite powerful world, they are a dragon. We might say that the imaginal realm is a realm that lives within individuals but above and beyond the material world, influencing it subtly but surely.

Since, from an elven point of view we eventually become what we think, imagine and do, our repetitive actions affecting our physical form through the lifetimes, eventually those who think and imagine and act like dragons (hopefully of the creative sort of Asian lore, rather than the destructive sort of western lore) will physically become dragons as well. We just hope that they actually enjoy it as much as they think they will. But if not, then surely, they will in time become something else.

Are we born to be elves?

The answer is yes, but not in the way that many folks would think. This question is similar to the one about being genetically elven, and as we've said, while some folks may be descendants of those upon whom the tales of elves are often based, not everyone from that genetic line chooses to pursue the Elven Way (in fact very few do) and not all those who pursue the Path of the Elfin are from that genetic heritage nor need to be.

But the question: are we born elves? is really a slightly different question. And we say yes, we are born elves not because of our genetic heritage but due to our spiritual heritage. We are elves because we choose to be elves and we choose to be elves because of who we are, because Elfin calls to us, because, quite often, we have been pursuing this path in various forms from one lifetime to another. We may not have called ours'elves 'elves.' We may have called ours'elves 'star children' or some other name but the reality of our being is the same.

And it doesn't matter what our ancestors believed or how they acted as individuals. It doesn't matter if they thought themselves elves or not, or even bothered to even consider the idea. What matters is that it calls to our own hearts and minds. And why does it do so? Because we are elves. Because this is what moves us, brings us joy, enlightens our minds, awakens our spirits and nurtures our souls. We were born to be elven and we sing the praises of the Divine Magic, of the stars of Elfin that this is so.

Our elven ancestors may or may not have been our genetic ancestors but they are most assuredly our spiritual ancestors and in the realms of Elfin, those wondrous realms of spirit and magic, this is what really matters.

"Most folks tell us they have two sides to them, a dark and a light, but we elves compare ours'elves to a huge box of crayons filled with colors."

Are all elves tall?

Tolkien is partially responsible for this idea that elves are tall, statuesque, all of us looking like fashion models but while this is certainly true of some elves, the traditions of the elves, found in our own and other's tales about us, including Tolkien, offer us a variety of elven sorts. We are not sometimes called the wee folk for nothing.

It is true that like faeries, this idea of making elves small was used by those who wished to diminish us in the popular eye, to make us little, cute and insignificant. However, it is simply too limiting to expect that all elves are tall or even beautiful in a socially acceptable way. We are a varied folk and come in all sizes. And we are in the process of becoming. We are elves and we are becoming ever more elven at the same time, becoming increasingly our true s'elves.

We, ours'elves, are inclined to think that we are all beautiful, but in saying that we are, more often than not, speaking of a spiritual beauty rather than traditional notions of what is beautiful. Our beauty often comes from our uniqueness. What makes the elven beautiful, most often, is that we are mysterious and exotic by nature. People sense that we are different than they are and even while that often arouses their superstitions about everything magical and occult, it also often intrigues them. Certainly, this is the case if they thems'elves have a bit of elfin in their own being.

And it should be noted that we elves tend to see beauty everywhere. We are, for the most part, less critical than many other folks, and much more accepting. We find a smile beautiful whenever it is sincere whoever is wearing it. So if you ask, are all elves beautiful? Then we'd answer: yes, we are! Although, those who are not elven may not agree with us. Certainly, those who judge us by traditional societal values may not do so. But then who are they to decide what is or isn't elfin. We elves reserve that right — the right to define ours'elves.

❧

Are all elves thin?

There is an idea that elves are all thin that is put forth in most stories and fairy tales, with an occasional exception (there is an overweight elf, if our memory is not mistaken, in some of the *Bordertown* novels and short story collections). We are also told by our elven grandson in the Ukraine, Nikolay Lyapanenko (see his recently published book *The Elves from Ancient Times to Our Days*), that elves being thin is a fervent belief of some of the modern Russian elves and we think, for the most part, it is a belief worth fostering in some ways.

We've spoken to this idea elsewhere in some of our books, and our opinion is simply this, that elves, for the most part, tend to be at a weight that is healthy for thems'elves as individuals (and this varies for each elf according to bone structure and other biological factors) and that allows them to feel attractive, for we elven very much like being attractive as much as we are able. We are, after all, enchanters.

Now, it is a fact of the modern world that in many places the diets that are offered us are not exactly conducive to being svelte, no matter how little one may eat. And it is a simple fact that once most individuals get a bit past forty, then gaining weight becomes increasingly easy, so that one needs quite a bit less food to eat. This perhaps is preparing us for a time when we will live as astral and etheric beings and need no sustenance of a material sort at all as Light Beings.

But this also means that most of us must exercise, watch our weight and follow a healthy diet, and that becoming or remaining thin is a bit of a challenge, but one that these elves have taken on for our own s'elves while passing no judgment upon others. For us, a love of things elfin and an aspiration to following the Elven Way, with a concerted effort to do so are all we require of those we nurture. It is our observation that if one truly wishes to be elven, one will begin to take one's health and thus one's weight into careful consideration.

We may also note that in our experience that Grimlens, those often fanatical and sometimes elven hating beings, also are often thin and hard bodied (while goblins tend toward overweight). Thus being thin is not, in and of itself, a sign that one is an elf. Only the pursuit of The Elven Way, of living one's life as an elf, is a true indication of elfinness and that, by its nature will incline one to be the best one can be on every level of manifestation.

"We sometimes say Faerie Awaits You, but that is not quite true. Faerie hungers for you just as much as you hunger for it and it is searching for you everywhere."

—*Words of the Ancient Ones*

Are elves healthier than other people?

There are some elves who think that we have more white blood cells than other people, and that we have to their minds a greater ability to heal. However, as is so often the case, they have presented no truly valid and reliable scientific evidence that this is so. Of course, we are not disputing that it may be possible for some elves or some people in general to have a higher white cell count.

At the same time, it should be noted that the vast majority of elves have a great interest in being fit and healthy and thus pursue those diets and lifestyles that tend to foster a healthier life. Do we always choose genetically superior bodies in which to incarnate. Perhaps not. Health is certainly a concern, but there are other spiritual issues involving our individual and collective destiny that affect the bodies and thus the genetic lineage we choose for a particular lifetime.

There are some elves who choose the path of the healing shaman or of the sorcerer who learns to navigate the inner interior of the soul, and for these individual elves it is often the overcoming of their own health issues that leads them to the wisdom to heal others. Silver Flame was very frail as a child and had bulbar polio at six years old. And now, reflecting back, she feels that it was simply part of her life path as a healer, an elven sorcerer, to overcome this personal affliction and the fear of death at such an early age. It was from the early experience as a crippled child that she learned the importance of compassion and looking deep within the person for the light that is within us all rather than the exterior characteristics and physical being, an understanding on her part that guided her path as a healer in both the psychological realms and spiritual realms. Elves come to this physical world to bring the light of elfin and also to learn their own lessons of the soul. Like all other beings, we are evolving!

So we say, the effort to lead a healthy life tends to get the best out of whatever body one may inhabit no matter what its genetic weakness and strengths may be. Just as one may inherit a very superior genetic makeup yet abuse it to the point of ill health and death, so may one do one's best with what one has and this, more than anything, defines the elves.

ॐ

Do elves age less quickly than normal humans?

This is a popular idea with writers and with those of us who are elven as well. We'd certainly like to think that this is true, and many elves, particularly when they are very young, seem to accept this idea. Alas, there is no genetic evidence that this is so, however, in our own experience we have noticed that elves do tend to appear younger than those who are not elfin who are our contemporaries.

If this is a genetic propensity, we don't really know. And as we said we have no evidence that this is so, we merely have our own experience and observation and we are inclined to think that this is less of a matter of genetics and pure material manifestation and more of a matter of spirit and soulful development. However, if yours is a strictly materialistic view of Life and the Universe then it cannot help but be a matter of genetics, just as our propensity toward and love of all things elven would thus be genetic. We call ours'elves elves, therefore, because we are genetically programmed to do so.

The idea that is often put forth that one is only as young as they feel, think, act, etc. does have an effect upon the elves. Not only do we often tend toward healthier lives, thus more attention to our diets and to exercise and taking care ours'elves in general, but we also tend to be less stressed than many of the folks about us. This is not to say that we never experience stress, but we know individuals, far too many individuals, who are not elfin for whom stress and anger and frustration are not an occasional occurrence but a life habit. They are always upset about every little thing that goes wrong in their lives and things always seem to be going wrong.

It is not that we elves don't age; clearly, or perhaps unfortunately, we do. Like most folks, we'd rather not. However, the idea of aging stresses us far less than it does most folks (and stress leads to aging). While so many others we have encountered are ever complaining about getting old, we're still smiling and that smile, more than anything, makes us seem much younger than we appear to be.

Do elves sweat?

We've heard that some people have put forth the idea that elves don't sweat. We suspect that they believe too that we don't have some other bodily functions that are essential to being in a human body. Alas, being able to sweat is a vital part of a healthy body for all humans (which includes elves), thus the idea that we don't sweat is rather counter to the idea that they also seem to hold that we elves are healthier than most other folks. If we are truly healthier than others, we'd probably sweat more than they do, not less.

However, if we remove this idea of not sweating from its essential materialistic view of elfinness and extend it, as we think nearly everything about elven nature should be extended, to a more spiritual, energetic point of view, then we could say and we'd quite agree that elves for the most part are rather more composed as beings than many other folks. We don't sweat the small stuff! We don't tend to get frazzled easily as so many others we've encountered around us do over every little thing and this may in part be due to the fact that we view life and development from the point of view of the stars. This is to say that we understand that most of what goes on in a particular life is transitory and that we have lifetimes yet to go upon our journey as well as having been on this Quest to manifest Elfin upon the Earth (and surely other planets and dimensions) for many lifetimes already.

So if that is what they mean in proclaiming that elves sweat less, we guess we'd have to agree with them.

"The elves say: If you need help going higher, lift others up."

Are all elves white?

Because the Scythians, from whom most Western tales of elves seem to originate and to whom most Western elven ancestries may be traced, had pale white skin (came from the Caucasus region and thus were Caucasian), red hair and green eyes, some folks seem to think that all elves must share these features to be elven. Naturally, those who believe this are either writers who are seeking to define elves for their fiction or individuals who have red hair and green eyes and pale skin who wish to use this to prove they are of elven blood in a world that is skeptical that anyone can be elven.

However, if we follow the work of Laurence Gardner (*The Realms of the Ring Lords*) and Nicholas de Vere (*The Dragon Legacy*), we are informed that the Scythians had tribal marriages and connections both to the Semitic peoples, thus Jesus is seen by them as being of the royal elven bloodline, and the Egyptians, as well as others; and it should be clear that elves would not be strictly of a particular body type, hair or eye color or skin tone.

Of course, some might argue that these other elven are not pure elven but that argument, of racial purity, which is used so often by various racists and intolerants everywhere to attempt to dignify their lunatic and hateful beliefs, holds no sway with the truly elven. We embrace our kin whatever their genetic heritage.

And we should remember that this idea of racial purity is really, for the most part, a relatively recent one and arises more from the national idea of race than the modern one of physical characteristics. This is to say that in the past when speaking of race, people spoke of the German Race, the Japanese Race, the

English Race, etc. and they are not speaking entirely of Caucasian, Asian, etc. which is a broader and more modern view.

If we look further we also find traces of elven peoples and civilizations in ancient history throughout all the world including: the menehune of Hawaii; Danavas, Gandharvas, Apsaras of India; and the Ainu of Japan.

And it is important to remember that in the past that for many tribal folk, being or becoming a member of the tribe could occur in numerous ways. One could be born into the tribe. One could marry into the tribe and one could be initiated into the tribe. All made one a full member of the tribe.

We elves, in this way, are thus a more tribal oriented folk. One can be born of the genetic line of Elfin, one can marry into the tribe, by which we mean become apart of us because of friendship and love, and one can be initiated into the tribe, which is to say love the elven and all things of Faerie so much that one is elven whatever body or genetic line one has chosen to be born within.

In the long run, however, the only true indication of who is and isn't elven is in the way they lead their lives. Do they follow the elven way? Then they are elven. It's that simple.

Are elves always androgynous?

It is true that compared to many other folks, particularly mankind and even orcs, we elves are inclined to be more attuned to both sides of our being. Which is to say that from Carl Jung's view, we'd be more in touch with our anima (for males) or animus (for females) than non-elven folks tend to be. Our males are in touch with their feminine side and our females in touch with their masculine side.

However, to say that all elves are androgynous in appearance simply is too restrictive and we elves, if anything, tend to defy most limitations and preconceptions about us. Elves are ever unique and varied so the idea that there may be extremely feminine elves or extremely masculine elves is not beyond the boundaries of conception, although we don't really tend (and tend is a word we use often concerning our people) to be extreme about anything, although sports might be an exception.

And that is the point really. With elves there is nearly always an exception, or several, until the so-called rule is itself the exception. For we are, certainly by our own reckoning as well as that of others such as those who love to tell tales about us, an exceptional people.

࿔

Do elves have enhanced senses?

There are some folks, particular writers of stories containing elves and also some of their readers, who would like to think that we elves have keener senses than most other folks do. And, in a sense, we agree with them, although they are inclined to attribute these superior sensory abilities (as they do to so much else about the elven) as an aspect of our genetic lineage. We, for the most part, find that we disagree with that assessment since we attribute elfin primarily to spiritual values, qualities of character, soul and magic rather than to physical aspects of being.

In our experience, if we have heightened abilities of a sensory nature, greater intuition, keener eyesight in some cases, increased hearing abilities, and other things, it is because we have on the one hand paid attention to these things, valuing them more than many others do and on the other hand because we don't have a tendency to engage in those things that dull the senses as so many folks do.

Most elves don't smoke cigarettes (or if we do we give them up in time) thus our sense of tastes is mostly unimpaired. We don't drink alcohol to extremes, or not very often, and thus most of our other senses are intact. And we tend to spend as much time as possible in nature, listening to the birds and the whispers of the tree and brook spirits, opening our senses in

the now. We are lovers of the light that radiates from all things and these are the energies upon which we concentrate our awareness and hold of highest value.

It is said that a blind person will develop hir (his/her) other senses to make up for the loss of hir sight and just in this way do the elves, by paying attention to our senses, instead of paying attention to most of the senseless gibberish of the world, use our own senses to their fullest extent. This is not an effect of genetic lineage, although we are not denying the possibility that some elves may have certain senses that are superior to others, including other elves, but that it is our actions and our behavior through life that mostly affects what we are and what we become. Nature (genetics) is but one part of the picture. Nurture (our environment and the way we've been raised/reared or as we elves say sometimes "blossomed") is another aspect to consider. But we elves have added another factor to the Nature/Nurture debate and that is the magical aspect, our choice to follow a particular lifestyle, which for us is the Elven Way (see our book of that title) and we might call this Nether for we are beings of the Nether realms with inner senses of perception that most don't even realize exist, born of our choice to be our own unique s'elves.

∼

Are elves hypersexual?

If anything, we elves may be hyper-sensual. We are very in touch with the sensual, feeling aspects of the world in all its various forms. Thus we tend to be more intuitive than many others, not because they are incapable of being intuitive but because they so often discount their intuitive feelings. What they tend to promote instead is what they call their gut feelings, but more often than not, this has little to do with their true gut feelings located in the Hara and everything to do with their inculcated prejudices and what they call feelings are really mind dominated emotions.

This is not to say that we are not sexual beings. But then most of humanity and in all life in general are sexual beings. What differentiates elves from many others is not our interest in sexuality but our lack of shame in being sexual and our rather open attitude toward sex and nudity. Unlike many other folks, we don't pretend that we are not interested in sex as they often do, for this pretense of lack of interest leads to perverse desires and behaviors all carried on in secret. This is the case with so many evangelists and politicians and other public figures who pretend they are happily married individuals who never have sex outside of their marriage who then have affairs, consort with prostitutes and have homosexual relationship while pretending to condemn homosexuality. Elves who are homosexual are seldom hiding in the closet, unless their lives depend upon it, they are out there for all to see. This is not to say that all elves are homosexual, surely we are not, or that all elves are hypersexual, but that elves are ever free to be what they truly are, and pursue their own interests and desires with mature and consenting others. As elves in striving to be more enlightened as beings, we are seeking not simply to be more conscious, but more sentient in our consciousness, more feeling aware, more in touch on a feeling level with the all of life. This is, in part, why we have such a compassionate feeling for the trees, the whales and the all of life. We are in the now, alive and feeling, bringing our spirit into matter. And this is why we often chant in our magic circles: "We have come to take our bodies to give our spirits birth."

❧

Do elves have facial hair? Are elves ever bald?

It would be pleasant from an elven point of view if we never went bald. In our imaginal states of being we are not bald. Deep in Elfin itself, we of course would not be bald either, or at least only by choice. For elves ultimately have shapeshifting abilities and through the course of time and evolutionary development will become what we wish to be, as we wish to be.

In movies, books and lore, the elven usually have long hair. In the modern world, this is not always the case, but again it is primarily a matter of choice. Elves may appear as they choose. The effects of the dark magic, by which we mean our manifestation in the material world during the Kali Yuga (which the Earth entered about 5000 years ago and will continue to be in for another 427,000 years), the dark age, the most materialistic age in which nearly everything is viewed from a material viewpoint, is that we are not yet fully in control of our bodies and our lives. But then, beloved kin, that is why we have come here, is it not? To gain power within the material realms in order to manifest Elfin in reality?

Some people view the Kali Yuga as being an age of darkness, by which they mean evil, and surely there is much that is wicked that is going on in the world, but from the elven point of view the Kali Yuga most of all signifies the material orientation. Thus in this materialistic age, many people judge elves solely by physical characteristics, like whether we have pointed ears or not, and many kindred make assertions to their elven natures based upon their genetic lineage to the ancient Scythians and so forth, by virtue of their elven bloodline. But ultimately it isn't having hair or not on our heads or faces, nor pointed ears, nor a particular bloodline that makes us elves. It is our own natures, our spiritual and soulful natures. It is a very simple fact that almost no one but elves loves elves and wishes to be elves and bothers to live their lives as elves but elves or those who have some elvish in them.

Tolkien apparently wrote (and we admit we are not experts on Tolkien's lore) that elves didn't have facial hair but then we were told he gave Cirdan the elven shipwright a beard. Elfin by its nature is protean, vast and of greater variety than most imagine. As we master the material world in time we shall become physically as we desire. But this will only come about in the long run from mastering our own inner natures, our psyches and our spirits in harmony with our soulful nature. Note the Australian television series *Cleverman* in which there is an aboriginal tribe whose members are faster and stronger than normal humans and are called 'hairies' because they are covered in hair. To our minds, these are just another tribe of elves.

While the material world surely has effects upon our attitudes and thus our spirits, it is the goal of every magic wielder to reverse this process and have a spirit so powerful it masters the material world. This is surely the case with nearly every great person who has ever existed and faced terrible obstacles in the material world only to overcome them in time with the power of their spirit. This is the idea conveyed when a warrior is told to never let hir enemies see that sHe is afraid. But our mastery of the material world has almost nothing to do with subjecting Nature or others to our will but is primarily about mastering our own s'elves, our own spirits, and thus from that our own bodies and our own realms of being, for from the world of spirit, the world of the Divine Magic, all things are born.

"Our bodies may age but our elven spirits are ever young. This is not just something we say but the reality of our true elfin nature."

—*Old Elven Knowledge*

Is there a point at which one is too old to be an elf?

From time to time, some young person sees a photo of us and thinks, how can they be elves? They're too old! Of course, they are influenced by Tolkien's writings and like to imagine that they are somehow immortal or near immortal as his elven characters are. Since their bodies haven't changed fundamentally since they reached their twenties, it is an easy thing to imagine that they might never grow old. However, in time, if they continue on this path, they will encounter the fact that none of us escape the demands of change that the material world places upon our physical bodies.

We elves are essentially spiritual beings, which is not to say religious beings, but beings whose essence is focused and derived from spirit and the underlying energy that the material world is formed upon, rather than the transitory nature of material manifestations. Spirit is being defined in this sense as energetic consciousness. When we come to realize this truth, we become more attuned to our true natures, which are energetic, and we begin to see beyond any particular lifetime, and thus beyond the illusion of transitory material form or existence.

We are elves with aging bodies. We are also ancient elves. More ancient than we appear no matter how old we may seem. In the not too distant future we will pass from these particular bodies and find new material forms for manifestation. We will still be ancient elves. Even more ancient, but not by much, and surely not as ancient as some of our kindred. But, as the physicists like to say: It's all relative. And as we elves like to say: How about another dance!

☙

Are elves politically liberal?

Being politically liberal minded folks ours'elves, we'd like to think that all elves are liberal, but that simply doesn't accord with our experience. This, alas, is a tendency that many elfin folk have when thinking about the nature of elves, which is to say, we tend to assume and think that all elves and elfae (elven, elfin, faerie folk of various sorts) are all like us. Thus if we are tall, we may think all elves are tall, or we are skinny, we may think that all elves are also so and so on. This is not to say that there are not stories and lore that we can base these ideas upon, but even then, just because someone wrote something about our people in a story, doesn't make it so for all elfin folk. It is important to remember that most stories about elves are not actually written by the elven and are based upon the experiences of their world and not necessarily ours.

The truth is that elves are many things, myriad and individual and eccentric and varied in ways that is hard to even imagine. Almost anything we might say about elves, you're likely to find an exception to the rule, but elves are the exception to the rule, except for those of us who are hiding ours'elves by conforming, in order to protect our people and carry on our lineage in secret in case of persecution, which alas, is not unknown to elves. Even today, when things are for the most part more tolerant, there are still those who frown upon and ridicule our existence. Which is really for the best, since if they actually believed we existed they'd find some reason for being prejudiced against us. Thus, wise elves are not prejudiced, we've suffered too much of that ours'elves to participate in such folly.

But, again, as much as we'd like to think that all elves are liberal folk, our experience tells us this is not so. The elven culture attracts all sorts of folk, conservative as well as liberal, libertarian and probably communist, certainly socialist and it is not for us to say who is or isn't an elf, nor is that the right of anyone else. Of that, we are certain, if of nothing else concerning elves. Are all elves kind? We'd like to hope so, but alas, the Unseelie folk are not always kind and caring. Are all elves compassionate? We try to be but are not always successful at this ours'elves so how could we demand it of others. Are all elves beautiful? Well, surely in their own way, although the physical form doesn't always reflect the beauty of the spirit and vice versa. In a certain sense what makes elves beautiful, besides the imaginings of others, is not our face or our form but our magic.

Still, we expect that for the most part you will find that most elves tend to be liberal minded and that the conservatively or exclusively oriented are generally less inclined toward our culture. We have our divergences as a culture just like any other, but really even more so. What tends to unite us is our love of magic and of all things elven.

It is true that there are those who would like to tell us what constitutes being an elf in a fairly rigid fashion and along some decidedly limiting parameters. But those for the most part are being influenced by their life among man and other, even less kind, kinds. And as they explore deeper and deeper into Elfin, if they do in fact persevere upon this path, they will surely have experiences that will open them up and expand their consciousness and awareness.

This we can say for certain, that one cannot pursue the Elven Path for long without attracting the attention of the Shining Ones, the higher elfin spirits that guide us and they will always arrange for us to have those experiences that open our hearts, our minds and our spirits. In the gentle time, all we can do is encourage our kindred as best we may, accepting them for who they really are and as they present thems'elves as being for the moment and encouraging them to accept and embrace all sincere kindred as their own no matter what our temporary and transitory political beliefs may appear to be. Nothing influences people like love and acceptance.

൙

Are Elves Nature Spirits?

There is a tendency for some folks to represent elves, and faeries in particular, as being nature spirits, tending to gardens and trees and the other aspects of nature as, say, the flower fairies are seen as doing. (By the way, we love the flower fairies. When our daughter was growing up we had the flower fairy alphabet upon her wall to help her to learn the alphabet, or as we sometimes call it, the aelphabet.)

And the truth is we elves are nature spirits, if by that you mean that we are natural born elves, living in a natural world, attuned with Nature as much as we are able and living in harmony with Nature as well. Do we tend to gardens? Take care of the trees? And do other things to promote the life of

Nature in the world? Why that depends upon the individual elf.

Of course, sometimes when people say that we elves are nature spirits, they mean we elfae are imaginal representations of or metaphors for the forces of Nature somewhat anthropomorphized. While it would be accurate to say that some of us truly are a 'Force of Nature,' we've known elves of this sort, we are not really elementals or aspects of Nature represented in human form, except in the sense that all beings are a part of Nature and we elfae surely are as well.

The idea that some folks hold that they are apart from Nature, or even worse that they are above Nature and thus can exploit it, make profit from it and destroy it at will with no regard to its own life or spirit, is surely not an elven point of view. And in that sense we are definitely Nature Spirits as opposed to whatever they happen to think they are. The Chosen of their particular Demigod, usually, divorced from Nature apparently or to their minds never apart of it at all, forever at odds with Nature and determined to dominate it as they are determined to dominate everything and every one around them, exulting in their own ignorance as they do so and totally unaware or discounting their utter dependence upon Nature.

We elves are permanently married to Nature both here on Earth and among the Stars. We are soulful spirits expressing our s'elves through Nature and quite joyous about our relationship to it, ever seeking to improve our connection and increase the harmony between us.

"We elves don't worships gods, we commune with Nature which is Divine and Magical."

Chapter 4:
Elven Awakening

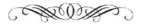

> Perhaps the most lonely, difficult and yet ultimately energetic time in an elf's life is the beginning period of an elven awakening, when first becoming aware that one is some 'other than human' and different from normal humans around hir. This chapter is particularly written for our brothers and sisters who are in this process and it explores questions we are often asked about an Elven Awakening, as well as some questions requiring a deeper exploration about the elves who have already awakened and begun consciously living with an elven identity.

How important is the Awakening compared to Perseverance of the Elven Way?

A lot of emphasis is given among the elven and the elfae to the significance of the Awakening, which is to say one's first realization to the depth of one's being that one is truly an elf or other. Less attention, however, is given to the significance of perseverance on the path although in the long run this is much more important. This is perfectly understandable since the Awakening is often quite dramatic in its manifestation. It makes an impression on one that one is unlikely to forget easily.

The Awakening often involves signs and omens (although the path itself, which is to say the pursuit of the path and perseverance on the path often also have many signs along the way) and even more than that, the Awakening often involves aspects of one's unconscious that have laid dormant all one's life awaiting those signs to occur. The Awakening evokes aspects of the Collective Unconscious and memories of one's previous lives. Rather like trigger words or phrases that are used in hypnosis that spark a particular behavior or reaction in the individual, these signs or events instigate one's awakening and for some this can be quite emotionally astounding as well as transformational.

However, the effects of the Awakening that can be so profound for many of us, even resonating in our lives for months or years to come, don't last forever. Like newborn babes we arrive in the world hungry for more, eager to connect with our kindred (often it is our kindred who helped awaken us) and to live fully in the world as the elves we know ours'elves to be. But alas, what we frequently encounter is a dearth of feedback and a world that often seems determined to deny us our heritage and our chosen identity.

Even those who seemed like our good friends previously are often astounded and disturbed by this sudden change in us, particularly in many cases making fun of or refusing to even use our newly chosen or given elven name. They frequently accuse us of having joined some cult and we, for our part are often chagrined by their negative reactions, wonder why they haven't awakened as well, and wonder, if we've joined a cult, where are all our cult members? Not only do we usually lack a charismatic leader to empower us, as one would find in a cult, we lack the peers in our vicinity who would reinforce our new found beliefs.

Still, this is for the best. We would never wish our blessed elfin culture and magic to be turned into a cult and every true elf tends to reject cults because we have such a propensity to question (rather than just believe and accept with wide eyes and slack jaws), which in our experience drives both the cult members and the charismatic leader crazy. We tend to get harassed in cults and told we just have to have faith. We do have faith. Faith in our own true s'elves, faith in logic and reason, and faith that we will in time find our very own kin.

It is at this point when we find there is so little of our culture available to us and seemingly so few elves to help reinforce our new understanding of ours'elves that perseverance kicks in or, as is the case with many elves, we fall back into the world, or sometimes just limp along half starved of the elven energy, companionship and magic that we so desperately yearn for and need. And, alas, while we thought the world would suddenly change around us, this world seldom changes quickly, we've found, and when it does it is seldom a good thing. Instead, it plods on in its insane and haphazard fashion, in its manic depressing way, with benevolent evolution taking far more time than we ever imagined. Often those kindred we encountered and who helped initiate our Awakening turn out to be just other elves struggling as we are to find thems'elves, survive and succeed in the world, and due to our rather migratory nature, ofttimes they just wander elsewhere.

In many ways, Awakening while impressive and profound for many of us, is not nearly as important as the ability to persevere on the path. There is a necessity for a sort of s'elf starter aspect to being an elf. One needs to continue on even though one is alone, or there are only a very few others about one, or those that one interacts with are mainly online and at a distance. Many will fall away, lose interest, be attracted by this or that fad, but many will also return in time, drawn back by the love they felt among us and the truth that they cannot deny that lives even within their own souls, that they are elven true and we are their very own.

~

What are the different modes of Awakening?

The Awakening, the realization that an individual has that one is other than what one has been told one is nearly one's entire life — particularly the realization that one is elfin, elfae, or other of some sort — can manifest in a variety of ways. For many, it is a quite dramatic moment when it seems as though one has waited one's entire life for the message that one is elfin and that one's life from thenceforth will change forever, which it in fact does, however, usually not as quickly as one might wish or imagine. For it is the elfae who have changed while the world has remained the same.

For others, the Awakening is more subtle and sometimes even slower, a gradual realization rather than a sudden Awakening. Some encounter things, like *the Lord of the Rings* books and movies and just say to thems'elves, that's what I am, I'm an elf, or whatever it happens they may be. Some have told us that it was a song they heard that touched them to the depth of their souls and awakened them. Others are impressed by meeting those of their own kind, being so moved by these unusual being who accept one rather than incessantly tease, criticize and harass one, one says to ones'elf, "These are my people!"

Surely, many of us have Tolkien to thank in part for our awakening, although those of vampire heritage (what we'd call dark elf or unseelie blood), and Therians, werewolves and others of that sort, often have other authors or films that touched their beings. Tolkien made elves real for the elven. His writings told us that the elven are not mere etheric or ephemeral beings, but beings, however advanced, who were real flesh and blood like us.

Of course, Tolkien for his part was inspired by other writers, such as Lord Dunsany who wrote *The King of Elfland's Daughter*, as well as being inspired by the ancient tales of the Saxons, Angles, Jutes, and various Scandinavian Viking tribes to which they were related, even while often being in conflict with each other. All those peoples perceived of the elfin as being both supernatural and manifesting upon the Earth as real people in addition to ascending into the higher realms of existence, the upper branches of the Tree of Life, as the Shining Ones do.

But nearly all of us elfae have spent a great deal of our lives feeling different from those around us. We may try to fit in or not. Sometimes we simply don't even bother trying. We are so weird in the eyes of others that in our own hearts, it's not worth the effort. Many of us just give up trying after a while because no matter how hard one may endeavor to fit in, one never feels quite comfortable among the normal folk. And they, for their part, are never entirely at ease around the elfae whom they instinctively recognize as different even when we camouflage ours'elves so well we appear to be, on the surface, just another one of them. We arouse something vaguely atavistic in their subconscious and try as the normal folk might they can never quite get over it. Although in truth, they seldom try very hard for they are ever eager to find others that they can scorn, ostracize and feel better than due to their own unacknowledged feelings of inadequacy. How can they accept us when they can't even accept their own s'elves?

However one awakens, one is still faced with dealing with the world in all its irrational insanity. And that is always made easier when we find each other and particularly find those who are of our own band or tribe or family. When that happens, it all begins to make sense and the reason and purpose for our existence becomes clear and we spread our magic into the world touching all who are open to it and awakening those who are ready.

༄

Once an awakened elf are you always an awakened elf?

We say no not necessarily, and yes in one's soul. An elven awakening is an awakening to one's true inner nature and the essence of whom we are. It is a departure from our preconceived ideas of ourselves that we have learned from external authorities (like parents, teachers, religion), as we made our way living and surviving in this mundane world. But elves have many varying degrees of elven awakening that can come at any age and it may be subdued at any time to pursue other paths. It all depends on what the elven soul needs in this lifetime at a particular time. Yet, we feel sure that one's elven nature is always within one's soul, always guiding each elf on some level, and we certainly always will love and bless our elven brothers and sisters, even many years after they have departed our company for other pursuits.

For over 40 years now, we have been awakened to being elves, real elves, living the elven way, and expressing in the world our elven identity. In all that time, we have seen many individual elves and even groups of elves come and go in the elven movement, as many give up their elven identity, at least for a time in their lives. There are a number of reasons individual elves leave their elven identity and take on different explorations of self. Often, it is just a natural course of development in that many people embrace being an elf at an early age and even though their elven soul is deeply touched, they still need to explore and discover what else is in the world. This exploration of identity can be difficult without trying on new costumes, customs and traditions that may even encourage one to leave the elven identity at home. This pressure can be very difficult for some elves and it depends on the true needs of the elf as to whether sHe will hide or even give up hir elven identity to join in with these other groups.

Of course, elves are always exploring new ways and ideas and we elves love to participate in a variety of gatherings of people united for peace and love and creativity, so this exploration does not always mean the elf will give up hir identity as an elf. For at any age that an elf is awakened, a soulful energy is released within us and then we may see spiritual groups that we have never thought of embracing before to now be enticing and beautiful. These elves, Zardoa Silverstar and Silver Flame, have enjoyed the company of many New Age, Occult, Pagan and Wiccan groups both before and after our elven awakening, and this is so still today. In many ways, an elven awakening makes one more likely to join into other spiritual groups and explore the beautiful world we live in, and one certainly does not have to give up their elven identity while doing this.

But we have seen that some elves find that there is just not enough acceptance and support from others for being an elf. Elves are often encouraged and happy to join other more traditional and established groups like the Pagan community or New Age Groups, which sometimes (although certainly not always) marginalizes their elven identity. Remember that many elves, and certainly this is true of we Silver Elves (and this is certainly a matter of personal choice among elves as some elves are Pagan and other religions), do not worship a deity or multiple deities so we are neither Pagan nor Wiccan in that sense, but we nevertheless enjoy at times ceremonies with Pagans (both traditional Western and Hindu or other groups) particularly when they have communion with nature spirits, and also with Wiccans (who combine Paganism and the practice of magic) as they do often perform healing magic in which we enjoy participating. And many of us will on occasion put our own elven identities aside to enjoy gatherings of Sabbaths. Still, for some elves, we can get a bit lost from our elven identity if we must put it to the side too long without acknowledgement of who we truly are as elves.

And some elves find that being an elf just does not support their worldly ambitions (yes, some elves are quite ambitious), as there is no money and little fame or even worldly acceptance in "Being an Elf" (unless you are in the movies as an elf character; we all love Legolas). Being a real elf is not a popular identity in this modern world (even though many like role playing games and assuming a gaming identity as an elf). We have known many brothers and sisters to have their dreams of creating an elf haven and efforts toward it just not "pan out," sometimes after attempting such a goal for several years, and so they go on to other ambitions and identities. We understand, as it is hard to stay on a path that has more intrinsic rewards than extrinsic ones. We understand all of these reasons for treading other paths and are always happy for our kin when they are happy with their new lives, new friends and new families.

That being said, we do have a few elven kin who we have known for many years, even decades, that have stayed with us on the elven path all this while, proclaiming their elven identity and looking to the Shining Ones for guidance and soulful embraces. To you, dear starry brothers and sisters, we say thank you for joining us and thank you for being so Awakened so long to your elven nature and for your commitment to bringing Elfland into manifestation. May the Shining Ones bless you and all elves.

⮞

What is a Reawakening?

We have spoken of Awakening, which is when someone realizes, often quite suddenly and frequently unexpectedly, that one is elven or fae or other of some variety, and elves are all about variety. We've heard and read many tales of various elves' experiences with their Awakening, but almost nothing is ever said about Re-Awakening, which is also an elven phenomenon. So what is Re-Awakening?

In a sense, every awakening is a re-awakening. How can that be? Well, everyone, or at least nearly every elf or fae who awakens, is awakening because of something that is deep within them. Memories of past lives sometimes flash before their consciousness. And often, not so much memories as feelings of our lives in the past or our elven heritage. We have been elves before. We have, in a sense, been elves forever and the Awakening is often just a realization of this reality.

One might wonder then why we don't just come into this life knowing, from the very beginning, that we are elfae of some sort, but there are several reasons why this doesn't often happen. First of all, it is a simple truth that the vast majority of us are just not advanced enough to have obtained continuity of consciousness and come into this life with complete recall of our previous lives. For most of us such memories are fragmentary at best, often fanciful and mixed liberally with imagination.

But there is also some significance to such forgetfulness and that is it allows us to encounter the world purely at first, with a fresh unprejudiced eye and as we've said elsewhere this initial encounter with the world often serves as a sort of inoculation for the elfae. We get a good doze of it and are thus protected from its madness.

In each life we come in anew, as our sages have often advised us to do, looking at the world with the eyes of a child, and we see the world as it currently is before we then awaken and remember and compare it to our previous and ancient lives as elves. Such comparisons usually are not favorable to the current state of the world, but we are always hoping that one day we will come into a world that is quite like our ancient elven realms or so close that our efforts to establish Elfin on Earth will bear great fruit.

But there is another sense in which we use the term Re-Awakening and that is concerning those Elfae who have wandered from the path and then returned with their faith renewed. They, in that sense, Re-Awaken their realization of their elfae nature. This Re-Awakening, as we said, is usually much less dramatic than their first Awakening in this life, or as we say, perhaps their first Re-Awakening in this incarnation.

Why they wandered from the path usually has to do with the fact that we elves are few and far between in the world at this time and these elves don't offer our kindred what they have often come to expect from the world they were raised within which is to say, rules, authoritarian leadership and preciseness. We tell people to think for their own s'elves, to create their own unique 'ealds' (elven home/space) and to decide for their own s'elves what they truly wish to be and inherently are. But as much as the newly awakened often wish for more directive guidance, it just isn't good for them in the long run. The habits (hobbits?) of the world will not serve them in Elfin.

Of course, there are those who just came to us in the first place because this, that, or some other book or movie about elves stirred some little part of them that is elfae. But in time their excitement faded and they lost interest and wandered off elsewhere looking to continue the thrill. This is rather and actually very much like relationships and romances.

We often begin relationships with a bang, so to speak, and everything is exciting in the beginning. But if we move toward commitment in any fashion, that is to say we strive to sustain the relationship, then the work begins. The thrill that initiated the relationship has often faded and the day-to-day effort to keep the relationship alive comes to the fore. Some folks when faced with this reality merely move from one relationship to another, ever trying to experience that thrill again.

And this is often the same with those who come to us through a fad. They loved the thrill but the effort to continue their life in Elfin is just too much for them. They are just not developed enough in their elfae s'elves to continue on their own and alas the support network that would help them do that just doesn't exist as yet.

But this does not bother these elves. We nurture all our kindred as best we may, when they first awaken, when they re-awaken and even, if they allow us to do so, when they wander off. We are ever here for them. Ever here for each and every one of you, dear sisters and brothers. But what we have to give and offer isn't always what people imagine or expect. We have but simple elven magic and blessings for you and they are ever freely given and you are always welcome to them and welcome here in Elfin.

"We are born elfin, but in this world it is sometimes years before we awaken and put a name to what we've always felt about ours'elves."

—*Ancient Ways of the Elven*

Chapter 5:
How The Silver Elves Are Alike and Different From Other Spiritual Practices

> Quite often, our kin have been involved with a number of other spiritual groups and practices before entering these elven woods. Thus, they have upon their arrival here with us many questions about how we are alike and different in both our practices and philosophical beliefs from other spiritual groups, spiritual beings, and magic practitioners. We explore these in this chapter, including: our relationship to Paganism, to an "Elven Faith," to Witches, and to Wicca. We also explore how we relate to various religions and about common spiritual beliefs like past lives and teraphims or spiritual statues.

What's the difference between elves and Pagans? Do The Silver Elves follow an "Elven Faith?"

Some dictionaries will tell you that pagans are simply hedonistic folks. Others may tell you that pagan is a term for anyone who doesn't follow one of the main religions, while it will describe paganism as polytheism. And this is the reality really that those of the Pagan religion merely follow a multiplicity of gods or goddess, or in choosing a particular one to relate to, they acknowledge that there are others that one can worship as well. Although, our Pagan ancestors while being tolerant of their own many gods/goddesses on their own pantheon, were not always so open minded about those gods/goddesses of others. In general, these elves have found that many of the Pagans we've encountered are quite a bit on the hedonistic side of things.

Hinduism is one of the main forms of paganism in the world, tolerating a variety of godheads and beings. It should be noted that early Judaism was also a polytheistic religion but moved toward monotheism, the realm of the exclusive and jealous one god, as did the Egyptians. And it is quite possible that it was because of their sojourn in Egypt that the Hebrews gave up their many gods. Elohim being a plural noun.

Of course, when most of us in the Western world talk about paganism we are referring to a Paganism that has taken up the abandoned and often destroyed religions and gods and goddesses of our own Pagan ancestors before Christianity came and both persuaded and forced itself upon them, like a suitor who when charm doesn't work resorts to rape. The Paganism that most folks in the Western world practice has a lot of magic in it usually and is often akin, although different from, Witchcraft. Wicca is often seen as a combination of these two, which is to say it is sometimes used to indicate Pagans who practice witchcraft or magic. Although you will surely find some who would argue with those definitions, but then you will find people who will argue with about anything. Still, for the purposes of this particular book as it is our own elven way of thinking, these are the definitions we will go by.

We have attended a number of Pagan gatherings in our time, although according to the above definitions they were really primarily Wicca gatherings for there was always a bit of magic and witchcraft going on at them. We elves get along quite well with Pagans for the most part, both Western Pagans and the Hindu one's we've known (we've been to some of their gatherings as well). But these elves are not inclined to worship any gods and while religion is a personal choice of every elf, we expect that most elves, while having a fondness for this or that god or goddess, don't tend to involve thems'elves in worship. Although, we must point out that we will attend their services if there's free food involved at some point, and we certainly always enjoy dancing with them in communication with the beauty of nature.

While the Elven Way is the spiritual Path of the Elves and one we Silver Elves have been following for over 40 years, it is not a religion and all elves are free to pursue whatever spiritual path they desire, or not as the case may be. We Silver Elves are magicians and follow no particular religious dogma and understand the world as a magical or miraculous phenomena, and that all beings, by pursuing their own true path, will become whomever they truly desire to be. The path of the Silver Elves is that of Love and Magic.

And though the Elven Way is not a religion, one could say that we follow an "Elven Faith" that is similar to the original modern "Faerie Faith" (before it was crystalized into a more religious form and became more like a Pagan tradition), but with our own beliefs and relationship with nature spirits and impromptu rituals. While we do not worship any gods or goddesses, we do believe in them as real energies and we have respect for all Higher Beings. We Silver Elves do not follow Pagan traditions and ceremonies, but instead (and we do not speak for all elves as we are a varied magical people) tend to be more shamanistic and evoke Elven spirits of nature (see our *An Elfin Book of Spirits: Evoking the Beneficent Powers of Faerie*) and the elven elementals (see our book *The Elements of Elven Magic: A New View of Calling the Elementals Based Upon the Periodic Table of Elements*) as helpers/partners in our magic for healing and enchantment, rather than worshipping elven gods/goddesses, even those gods and goddesses who some attest to have been part of our elven heritage from ancient days.

It seems to us that any elf awakened to being an elf would have no reason to worship another elf (although elves are free to do so if they wish), for an awakened elf understands that all elves are part of the Divine Magic. From our elven point of view, if in history elves where worshiped (for instance by the ancient Celts who were said to be weary of the supernatural power of the Tuatha Dé Danann, the people of the goddess Danu and some say the god Anu), it was not by elves but by those who had an association with elves and respected and feared them (see more on this is Chapter 6 in the section on the history of "Elven Faith").

Elves and magic are like bread and butter, we just naturally go together. Actually, we're even closer than that, for magic is to elves as important to us as our pointed ears, and perhaps to many even more so. While we don't always have pointed ears we do always have magic! Thus we have a natural association with witches, witchcraft and magic in all its forms. And while we don't involve ours'elves in wicked magics, we do know of them, have studied them and understand that we have a natural kinship with the Unseelie Fae even if we don't, or hardly ever, agree or pursue the same paths. They are our kin, even if they are like the type of kin who come to the family dinner and spout racism and prejudice and whom you tolerate because, well, like it or not, you're related. Just in the same sense that Luke Skywalker and Darth Vader are related but use the Force in different ways. There is ever a hope in our hearts that we might redeem them and ever a hunger in theirs to seduce and corrupt us to the dark side. After all, what are relatives for but to work to give us a balance in our lives?

ತಿ

What's the difference between elves and witches?

We Silver Elves and our sisters of the Elf Queen's Daughters of old always felt very close to witches and in fact the Elf Queen's Daughters declared on a number of occasions that they were elven witches and this was surely true. They felt a close association with the witchcraft movement of that time (mid 1970s) and were very close with Oberon Zell Ravenheart and Morning Glory of the Church of All Worlds. They were also friends with Alison Harlow of the Covenant of the Goddess, Zee Budapest of the Dianic Movement and other prominent witches of that period. In fact, all of the above were featured on various of the letters of the Elf Magic Mail, which the EQD sent out each week, three letters (the amount you could send for one postage stamp) for over a year.

We Silver Elves also knew all of the above individuals, although we only ever meet Zee Budapest in passing. On the other hand we had spent times in several of the homes of Oberon and Morning Glory and Alison Harlow and in fact our friend Valerie Voight wrote a wonderful letter of recommendation for us to join the Covenant of the Goddess but as it turned out we didn't pursue that, our path leading us elsewhere.

But while elves generally feel a kinship with witches, we also feel a link to nearly all magical practitioners. There are elven wizards, conjurors, mages, curanderos (magical healers), sorcerers, shamans, diviners and magicians. But, of course, we are particularly enchanters (see our book *The Keys to Elven Enchantment*) for enchantment is the main and primary magic of the elven and always has been both in lore and tradition and in reality.

In later years (we've known them for over forty years), the founders of the Elf Queen's Daughters and the inner sisterhood tended toward Sorcery in their magic interest and practice but we Silver Elves still pursue enchantment as our primary magic. But the choice of what magic to do, as with nearly everything else concerning elves, is up to the individual elf and hir own spirit and soul. If the elf lets hir natural attractions guide hir, she is bound to find in time the magic that is perfect for hir.

So while elves can be witches and do witchcraft, not all elves are witches and surely not all witches are elves. We did meet a woman one time who came to us for guidance and lessons on the magical path, who claimed that she was of witchbreed, that is to say born to be a witch. But even if that is so, and we don't doubt her, it is still a matter of choice. She pursued witchcraft because she loved and was attracted to it and choose to do so. Of course, one could argue that she was born to love witchcraft, that it is in her blood but still the choice of acting upon it is hers. Without that choice, without that decision to act, there is no true magic. If we are compelled to do magic and have no choice in the matter then we are not magicians but puppets to someone else's magic. Choose wisely, beloved kin.

☙

Is Christianity incompatible with being elves?

One might think so if one went by many old faerie stories in which elfin folk are repelled by and unable to enter churches or holy ground. This is not really different from the idea that our Unseelie vampire cousins cannot abide crosses or holy water. This is old propaganda but totally inaccurate.

According to Laurence Gardner in his Grail series and Nicholas de Vere in his Dragon Legacy, Jesus is from the royal elven bloodline and the original formulation of Christianity was much closer to the Elven Path. The Catholic Church, according to them, perverted the faith and in doing so set itself against elven kind. For the elves were and are the true guardians of the light.

For our own part, we have simply noted and experienced that being elven transcends any particular religion, which is to say that those who are attracted to the Elven Way come from a variety of religions and cultures. There are elves who have come from the Christian faith and some that still practice or at least believe in its basic tenets. There are elves who tell us they are Muslim. Elves have no problem with anyone's faith as long as they don't attempt to force it upon us. We don't care what you believe, only what you do, particularly in relationship to us and also in terms of the whole planet as well. And probably most religions, while not actually believing in our existence, don't really have a difficulty with the elves.

There are, however, fanatics of various faiths and they, by their natures, are incompatible with everyone else and every other belief. It is unlikely, in fact near impossible, for one to hold such fanatical beliefs and to also believe one is an elf. It is even harder to embrace such beliefs and be an elf. But then, the Universe constantly amazes us. It is, after all, a most miraculous and amazing place.

~

Can elves be atheists?

Generally speaking, elves don't tend to be atheists. It's not that there is a rule against it, of course. The only rule elves really have concerning religion is "choose the one you're interested in following or not and leave others to do the same." However, most elves who have chosen to accept a religion seem to be generally associated with one of the major ones, such as Buddhism, Christianity, Judaism or Islam in a sort of vague way, or, as is the case with the vast majority, are Pagans who follow various gods/goddesses in a friendly and usually casual fashion. There are even elves who have taken Tolkien's writings concerning elves and turned that into a religion. It all works for us.

But elves for the most part, don't tend to be atheists. Atheism is simply a denial that there are gods or goddess based not upon evidence, but a lack there of by those who do believe. Really, in that sense, elves would be more inclined, being scientifically oriented folk, to be agnostic, merely saying we don't have enough information to make a decision one way or another and suspend judgment until we do have enough data to decide.

We Silver Elves, however, do believe in all the gods and goddesses, and can logically demonstrate their spiritual existence, we just don't worship them. Since we elves believe in magic, believing in beings who are more evolved, more intelligent, more powerful than we is not a difficult stretch. In fact, we can look about us on nearly any day and find individuals who fit in that category. When you add the idea that these are supra-dimensional beings, you just have to ponder radio waves, ultraviolet and infrared spectrum of light to understand there are many things, in fact most things in the Universe, that we don't normally see, which can affect us. Radiation is surely one of these.

On more than one occasion when we attended one of the weekend soirees that our sisters of the Elf Queen's Daughters used to hold, we heard Arwen exclaim how she didn't like to have atheists around because they tended to scare away the spirits and the elementals. The magical spirits in their eald just couldn't stand to have them around, she claimed.

For our own part, we Silver Elves are not bothered by atheists. Their position makes no sense to us, but then, neither does the blind faith that so many claim is their source of belief of their particular demigod. But to us, as long as they don't poo poo the magic while we're engaged in it, they may *not believe* all that they wish. There are things they don't see, as well as, don't believe, but as long as they are friendly to the elves, which is to say are elf friends, it's okay with us. It just makes the mix more interesting.

※

Do elves believe in past lives?

Life is eternal. Energy can neither be created nor destroyed. However, the particular forms that energy takes are transitory and, in many ways, ephemeral. The energy that composes our beings is essentially stardust. This sounds poetic, but it is really a scientific fact. Although, from an elven point of view, it is both poetic and scientific. Scientists from our experience are often romantic little spirits.

Thus, the energy that is at the essence of our being is eternal and from a physical point of view, there is no reason why in the trillions of years of life the energy that came together once to create our being wouldn't eventually come together again. After all, we have forever. We have explored all this in a number of our books. *Faerie Unfolding* is particularly recommended.

But when we talk of past lives, what we really want to know is not if the material form that we currently inhabit has been before, we might say conglomerated previously, but that our essence — which most people think of as our soul but we elves would call our spirit — has lived previously, even if in fact as is most often the case, we don't necessarily consciously remember it having done so.

And so our answer is yes, we believe in past lives. Even more importantly, we believe in future lives. And more significant than that, we believe in the possibility of gaining continuity of consciousness, which is our ability to remember (more or less) through the lifetimes all that we have experienced, although that does seem a bit much. After all, we sometimes have trouble remembering what we did last week, or had for dinner yesterday, so remembering every detail from a previous life seems not only suspect, but unnecessary.

Of course, many of us are not trying to remember our previous lives so much as forget most of the follies we've committed and restructure our memories, as we often do about the dead, into a more exciting and pleasing tale, leaving out the nasty, cowardly and mean spirited bits that are not quite in keeping with our aspirations to be more perfect and powerful beings. Thus we say again, we believe in future lives. For a lot of what we've been through, we prefer not to remember or at least we'd rather forget and pretend we weren't capable of being so disagreeable or ignorant. Still, eventually, we must confront ours'elves for who we are as well as who we've been in order to clear away all karma from past lives, to set ours'elves free to create Elfin on the Earth and among the Stars, according to our Visions.

So, if you ask, have we lived before? We've lived always, dear kin. But the question is not so much about have we lived, but how well we've lived. It's a matter more of quality than quantity. And the question about past lives isn't really, have we lived before, but will we live again? And the answer once more is, we are made of stuff eternal and partake of its life, on a journey never ending and Elfin eternal and everlasting awaits us to bring it to life through our lives.

Do elves interact with teraphim?

Teraphim is a word that comes from the word tera for earth and phim meaning spirit or angel. The Semite of southwestern Asia, which included the Akkadians, Canaanites, Phoenicians, Hebrews, and Arabs, often had a teraph (singular) or teraphim (plural) in the form of statues that they interacted with and from whom they received prognostication. This was before they moved from paganism to monotheism and prohibited the images of God/Gods or in the case of Islam, also the Prophet.

It should be understood that these statues are very much like churches, temples, mosques and sanctuaries in that they are not really meant to be seen as the spirit but rather a dwelling place for the spirit. They are the spirit's body, so to speak, or its house, just as our spirits are housed in our bodies. These teraphim are often called household gods, but again, from an elven point of view they are not gods but spirits that one can relate to and interact with. They might be compared to a form of psychic Skype.

The religions that have come to be against such communication with these spirits tend to see this as idolatry and condemn both the use of idols to portray their god and are generally against witchcraft and magic of any sort unless it is done by their god or as a consequence of an appeal to their god. On the other hand, the Catholic Church, one of the main sources of the Inquisition and the persecution of witches (although Protestants and Moslems also condemn witchcraft and magic), loves symbolizing Jesus on the Cross and has innumerable pictures and statues of saints with which one can interact. These statues are another form of teraphim.

This reminds us of the news story we saw going around the internet just a while ago about a woman in Britain who had been praying to a statue of Elrond for over a year thinking it was the statue of a saint. Well, of course, it was a saint, just an elfin saint rather than a Christian one but we're sure that her prayers got to where they were meant to go, as well as creating an echo in Elfin.

For our own part, these elves have over 500 teraphim in our humble abode. Most of these are elf figurines, but we also have gnomes, leprechauns, menehunes (pronounced may – nay – who – knees), brownies, faeries and we even have a few friendly dwarves, hobbits and trolls. We consider them to represent not only spirits that exist in the more etheric realms of Elfin and Faerie, but also to symbolize many of our kindred who are out in the world. For us these statues are a sort of astral and psychic telephone by which means we can easily connect with and bless our many kindred. Our book *Eldafaryn: True Tales of Magic from the Lives of the Silver Elves* has a great deal more upon these beings and our relationship to and interaction with them.

But let us just say for now that we love these beings. We love the statues and even more we love the spirits and people that they represent. We also have photos of our children and our parents and we also love both the photo and even more so our beloved kin that the photo represents. If we know you, beloved elfin, then while we may never have met we keep you in our hearts and minds always and while you may live at a far remove you are also here with us, ever and always.

Do elves interact with Genii Loci?

The Ancient Romans believed in and interacted with Genii Loci (plural), or Genius Loci (singular), the abiding and protective spirit of a place. This belief, however, was not exclusive to the Romans and was a widespread understanding that still exists today in the form of the idea of haunted houses and restaurants or other places having a particular ambience or spirit.

Elves and fae folk in general have long been associated with various wild places and in particular seen as protective spirits of certain forests, streams and springs. This is not entirely different from the idea that faeries are often protectors or caretakers of flowers or other growing things. And that we fae folk could with a wave of our hand either bless or blight livestock or crops. This idea was extended, as elves and fair folk in general were increasingly seen as elements of fantasy, to witches and their ability to bless or ruin crops. And during the inquisition, one of the many accusations about a particular woman accused of witchcraft was that her neighbor's crops failed or their cattle fell ill.

For our own part, these elves relate to the various spirits of whatever place we may be. We typically greet the trees each day as we see them, often bidding hello to the Faerie realms through them, saying, "Good morning, Faerie," or well, not morning, we are seldom up for morning, but surely, "Good afternoon, Faerie," or "Good Evening." We also greet the birds and the other creatures we may encounter. When we used to live out in Makaha (often referred to here on O'ahu as the Wild

West) in a valley between two mountains, we'd greet the mountains each day. However, these were old mountains, formed from volcanic ash, and every six months to a year someone would go climbing on them and fall to hir death, thus voluntarily offering their lifeblood to these ancient spirits.

There might be a tendency for many people to picture the spirit of a mountain as being separate from the mountain, and in the sense that we are spirits that live in humanoid elven bodies but are not those bodies, this is true for those spirits of the mountain as well. At the same time, the mountain is the spirit in the same sense that our bodies are a vibrational manifestation of our spirits and while we might be separated from each other, and surely will in time, while we inhabit these bodies we are one. (See our book *Eldafaryn: True Tales of Magic from the Lives of the Silver Elves*.)

Thus these elves are ever aware that we live in relationship to and in association with the spirit of the place where we currently abide and which forms the living body of our realm of Elfin that we call Eldafaryn. We also, when we go traveling, carry stones that we've painted sigils upon and instilled with magic to leave as gifts for the genii loci of the various realms we are passing through. It is, after all, from an elven point of view only courteous to bring gifts when visiting others. Hoping in this way to gain the friendship and blessing of the spirits of those realms.

We are, of course, animists seeing the life in all things, just as the physicist understands that everything is composted of atoms and energy, we understand that everything is indeed alive with its own vibration, nature, experience and inclinations. As elves, we ever seek to be on friendly terms as much as possible with everyone.

Are the Elves the same or different from the Djinn?

Djinn, who are sometimes called Genies, are usually spirits of the wind and fire but truly can come in any elemental form for they are inspiring spirits of Nature. Thus the word genie and genius are related. In that form they are sort of Muses from the astral and etheric planes of being. In as much as this is so, they are similar in some ways to the Shining Ones, although the Shining Ones are most often conceived of as being similar to Angels and in this inspirational form as Guardian Angels, while Djinn are often conceived of as being a variety of demon (see Jonathan Stroud's great *Bartimaeus* trilogy books, although there are actually four books in that series.)

Thus, in as far as the Shining Ones are advanced elfin, which is to say elves that have evolved to higher states of spiritual and etheric being, we have a certain similarity to Djinn. And in as far as we elven are conceived as a form of elemental, as say Gnomes are often said to be earth elementals, or sylphs to be air elementals, and undines to be water elementals, then there is a sort of association there as well. How salamanders came to be the elemental of fire in this sequence, we find curious, however, since salamanders, worms, snakes, etc. are all related to dragons, then this makes a certain sense.

And perhaps, in as much as elves are not always perfect beings and, in fact, can be quite powerful but not necessarily good (the unseelie), we might find some association with the dark and demonic forces, as Galadriel would have become if she had accepted the One Ring. In that light, we could find a certain relation to elves and Djinn as well. However, while there are similarities and associations since the all of life and the Universe is connected, elves are not Djinn, nor Djinn elves.

At the same time, from an elven point of view, all of us are in a process of evolution and all spirits, including the Shining Ones, have evolved and develop from more primitive forms to more complex forms and spirits. Unlike the idea that is usually held about Angels that they were created as is and are never changing, we elven assert that the whole Universe and every spirit within it are in the process of becoming (see our book *Faerie Unfolding: the Cosmic Expression of the Divine Magic*). This means that we have been through plasma states of being, of being minerals, crystals, rocks, etc., and flora and fauna and humanoid form and advance into the more spiritual and etheric realms becoming ever more powerful and conscious. So, once again, there is a link between elves and Djinn, particularly as magical beings, but then there is a link between elves and all being, especially those of a magic nature.

ॐ

What do the elves think of the Illuminati?

There is a lot of conspiracy nonsense about the Illuminati. It is particularly ridiculous since the illuminati is supposedly a secret organization and those who write about it are not a part of it nor really know anything about it. This is not to say that conspiracies don't exist in the world or that there are not those who call themselves the Illuminati and involve themselves in conspiracies to control mankind, the governments and peoples of the world.

Such conspiracies by the rich and powerful to control the general populous, as well as the economies of the world, and even other rich and powerful individuals and groups that are not a part of their circle, have always existed. That's mostly what war is about, gaining economic advantage and power over others. It is sometimes disguised as an ideological conflict or a religious dispute but behind that there are always greedy people seeking to exercise power over others and ensure their own continued place of privilege in the world or to establish such a place for themselves.

And it is likely that these groups and conspiracies will continue to exist for thousands of years into the future if they don't, in fact, lead us all to destruction. That some of these groups may call themselves the Illuminati is surely possible. We don't really know. That many of them think of themselves as the Illuminated Ones who are far above common humanity can surely be taken for granted. It is pretty obvious that this is the case.

However, it is important to understand that just as someone may call themselves a Christian or some other religious designation but not live up to the precepts of that religious philosophy, which seems to be the case with the vast majority of those who claim to be spiritual, or someone may make claim to being enlightened even though they are far from it, so too people may call themselves the Illunimati and not be illuminated at all. Quite the contrary.

The true Illuminati are not an organization at all really. They are the Shining Ones, the advanced elfae spirits that look over us and guide us and do all that they can to nurture and inspire us. And on our own plane of manifestation there are surely elfae of various sorts who, for their own part, are working ceaselessly to help and inspire our kindred in everyway that they can and do everything within their power to awaken the elfin and manifest Elfin upon the Earth. These individuals, while surely limited elves due to the constraints of manifesting in the material world and their own struggles as spirits and souls, are still, however, true members of the Illuminated. Which is to say they are truly enlightened elfin beings using their life and magic to do all that they can to aid us.

That others might call themselves the Illuminated is of little importance. If they are acting out of greed and purely out of self-interest then they are not among the Illuminated Ones. If they are seeking to control humanity for their own profit and most often out of a need to feel superior to others because of a lack in their own souls, then they are not enlightened they are merely tools of the demonic forces that control them through their emotional needs and psychological drives. They are still undeveloped souls like most of the rest of us. It doesn't matter what they call themselves, their magic, their actions are all that is really important and designates those who are truly enlightened, those individuals who are indeed Illuminated, and thus of the Illuminati, which is not an organization but a reflection of the reality of spiritual development and evolution.

"The elves are involved in an ongoing conspiracy to make the world a better place using love, magic and beauty as their tools."

—*Ancient Elven Knowledge*

Are elves related to Devas?

Devas are beings in the Vedic Philosophy who are seen as benevolent but in Zoroastrianism are viewed generally as being evil. Essentially, they would be equivalent to angels, thus the angels that serve the gods by helping humanity in Vedic lore and who are seen as fallen angels in Zaroastrianism. This is similar to the fact that horned gods are generally revered in Pagan worship but are seen as demonic by Christians.

For the elven, of course, Devas are essentially the Shining Ones under another name. And just as we elves may call ours'elves by various names: star children, flower children, space gypsies and so forth, so do the Shining Ones have a variety of names they've been called by different peoples around the Earth and elsewhere. This is not much different from the fact that in Tolkien Imladris, the secluded mountain resort of Elrond, Arwen and their elf kin, is called Rivendell by outsiders. Or the fact that Nihon is commonly called Japan in the modern world, outside of those who live in Japan (Nihon) and speak Japanese.

To us, the Shining Ones are essentially advanced elves, who have gone beyond the need or perhaps interest in manifesting in the gross material world, just as angels are advanced beings for the normal folk. Although, in their philosophy the angels have always been angels and mankind will always be man, whereas, we believe that the Shining Ones where once elves like us, who evolved through the various stages of development in this world and have gone on to greater things.

The elven view of life is one in which we are continually

learning and developing as spirits. We go through the stages of mineral life, flora, fauna, humanoid life and beyond. We are always, in a sense, elves, but we have been elven rocks and crystals, elven trees, elven birds, wolves and many other things. This is surely in part why we are so shamanically oriented as a people. We do not separate ours'elves from Nature, nor have we forgotten our sojourns among animal life. And because of that we are able at times to summon up the spirit of those beings that we have been, that still live within us in our unconscious or collective unconscious and can thus ride in the bodies of hawks or panthers or whatever form to which we've been associated and which often serve as our totems in our current life.

This same energy enables the Shining Ones to overshadow us at times, enlightening and inspiring us and occasionally urging us this way or that to do this or that thing for our own betterment and for the benefit of all. Although, they too must deal with the limitations of our current being and consciousness, just as a mage must manifest within the limitations of a hawk that sHe overshadows.

Life is continuous and related. Thus the Shining Ones, the elven devas so to speak, are not separate from us in the sense of being of an order of manifestation that we can never obtain nor aspire toward as the angels are viewed by most of humanity, but are seen by us as our parents, older brothers and sisters, and cousins, whom we model in many ways in developing our own behavior. Each of us shall one day be Shining Ones, although, certainly for these elves at least, that day is far, far in the future and many lifetimes yet to come. In the meantime, however, we do our best on each and everyday, in our relationships with each and every one and that is truly the surest path toward enlightenment and elevation/evolution to the realms of the devas and thus into the more etheric realms of Elfin.

≈

Is the sphere of Netzach specifically related to Elves?

Netzach on the Qabalahistic Tree of Life is the realm of Victory and particularly of victory over ones'elf, of rising above ones'elf and transcending one's limitations. Netzach is a sphere of long-suffering, of enduring to completion or therefore patience, and of strength. It is often related to the planet Venus and to enchantment and thus in all these ways it is very elven in nature.

But then one could, just as easily find aspects of elfin and the elvish personality in all the other spheres on the tree of life. That, in fact, is what the tree is for, to view life from its fundamental aspects. (see our book *The Elven Tree of Life Eternal.*)

If we took some of Tolkien's elven characters we could easily see Legolas and Tauriel (Peter Jackson's creative invention in the Hobbit), Thranduil, Elrond and even Galadriel in their warrior forms as being associated with Geburah, the sphere of Mars. Or we could take Elrond and Galadriel in their wisdom aspect as being associated with Binah, or in their occult knowledge aspect as being associated with Hod (Mercury) or Yesod (Moon) or perhaps the path between them. There is no sphere on the Tree, in fact, where one couldn't view elves in one of our many manifestations and characteristics. Just as elves would live, explore, roam and adventure in all parts of our forest, just as one knows every part of one's home or neighborhood, so do we, as elven, have a place in every sphere and path of the tree.

☙

Are Elves New Age or different?

We often hear people use the term New Age or New Agey in a rather condescending way, as through anything that is New Age is to be discounted as inferior or unreliable and not of the profound substance of whatever it is that they do believe in and which they are so certain is true and right because they believe it. However, when we ask these individuals to define what exactly they mean by New Age, they are never able to do so. They give us vague terms that simply reiterate their prejudices and distain.

We expect that this is true in part because there is no exact definition of what constitutes New Age thought or practices, which seems to include a variety of spiritual and religious beliefs that encompass the notion of the evolution of the soulful and spiritual nature of all beings and a general tendency toward globalism as opposed to the provincial and nationalistic outlook that so many currently hold.

In that sense, we elves are very much New Age for we deeply believe in the evolutionary nature of Life and see the Earth and its peoples and creatures in a holistic fashion. That these ideas are not really new but quite ancient is another aspect of our culture that is in keeping with most of what is

New Age. We are both ancient and modern. We honor the ancestors by honoring those around us, for we know that our ancestors have been reborn in our kindred. We carry our ancient culture within us, in what Jung would call the Collective Unconscious, and we revise it, recreate it and make it anew in our own lives.

That so many use the term New Age in a derogatory fashion is only to note that those who cling to the past often deride the new, for the new and different often scares them. When an elf awakens to hir true nature and takes on an elven name, it is not uncommon for those around hir, even hir friends, to make fun of it and resist using it. Change frequently frightens people. And let's face it, change can be very scary particularly if you resist it in all its forms and then it winds up forcing itself upon you.

But we elven not only attempt to embrace change regularly, to learn new things and new ways of being and doing, but we are in a continual quest to create change, to make the world a better place for all of us, to manifest Elfin upon the Earth. This is why we often speak of the Dawn of Elfin and the Awakening of the Elves. To our minds, the new age to come is an Elfin Age, an age of mutual tolerance and rampant creativity. And we awaken each day embracing the first light of that New Age that lives within our hearts and minds and is beamed from our eyes above our knowing elven smiles ever ready to be born anew in the magical light of Elfin.

Olde Elven Saying: "The time is always now."

Chapter 6:
The Past and Future of Elves

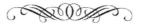

> Much has been written about the history of elves in legends and myths worldwide. Here we will give you our own thoughts on the questions people have about the history of our modern elven people and our Elven Faith, particularly as it defines who we elves are as magical beings, as well as who we will become in the future. We also take a glimpse into the future of our people on this planet.

How far back in history do elves and the original "Elven Faith" go?

We are not sure who first coined the words "Elven Faith" but the first time we heard it used was only a few months ago when Candace Apple, owner of a fantastic esoteric store, the Phoenix and Dragon Bookstore in Atlanta, Georgia, mentioned that she was planning to have in her store a special bookshelf for "Elven Faith."

We certainly must go much further back in history than the Celts to find the original Elven Faith, and this is near impossible to do with any specifics because it predates written history. The earliest elven spiritual practices were most likely shamanistic in nature and predated all religious beliefs, including the Celtic Faith, or Paganism from which much Neo-Paganism descended (although Neo-Paganism sprung anew from ancient traditions from all over the world). Legends show that the Celts related to the fairies and elves as being part of the spirit world, as life and nature around them, and made offerings to them via propitiation (see the works of Lawrence Gardner and Nicholas De Vere). The Celts perceived the elves as a sort of force around them and called them the "good neighbors" because they wanted to relate to them in positive ways. But the Celts did not see themselves as elves, and instead saw themselves as a separate race from the elves, from the Tuatha Dé Danann who they saw as a supernatural powerful people. In a certain sense the Norse were closer to the elves or being elven in spirit than the Celts, because much like Tolkien does in his fiction, the Norse believed that some of their people could become elven by achieving greatness.

The shamanic faith is a faith in magic and a faith in the ability of each person to use magic to change and affect their lives and the world around them without worshiping, praying to, or propitiating deities (see Sir James Fraser's *The Golden Bough*). In ancient Eastern spiritual practices, we also find this elven view and understanding that we are the Creators of our own reality. For example, this is continually mentioned in *The Tibetan Book of the Dead*, a funerary text that is a guide through the intermediate state (or bardo) between death and rebirth. In it, liberation is outlined to be achieved by recognizing our own ability as Creators and oneness with the Divine Energy. A very elven view indeed, particularly when understood in a magical sense!

Almost all lore that talks about faeries and elves says we are the Eldar race, most likely the first people to arise as a civilization. Thus we elven are associated with pre-written history and the idea of Atlantis and the Land of Mu. At the same time, Fraser's twelve volumes of research shows that the very first spiritual practices of people on earth were shamanistic, predating written history and religions. So if we elves are the first people, we are shamanistic people not religious people. Our ancient faith or spiritual practice was one in which we used magic to affect the world, and it was later in history that priests came and the religions of the world were created. Intermediaries with the spirit world, the idea of Gods/Goddesses, and so forth, including Paganism, all came later than our earliest elven spiritual practices that where shamanistic in nature.

Similar to the early elven spiritual practices, we Silver Elves can say that for us our modern Elven Faith is not a religion of any sort but more kin to shamanism, to viewing ourselves as one with Nature and the Divine Magic.

Are elves from Pleiades?

There are some folks that think that the elves came from the Pleiades constellation of stars. This is particularly so because the Pleiades are alternately named the Seven Sisters and because of our seven pointed elf star one can see how we elves love that idea. There is surely some mystical association there and an imaginal and mythical one as well. It stirs the imagination and gives us a sense of power and worth.

Others we've encountered are of the opinion that we came from Sirius. And still others yet write that we have an association with long dead star systems that died out on their own that forced us to migrate, or were destroyed by evil forces, sending us fleeing in various directions. Wicked forces that, to their minds, stalk the galaxies seeking us still.

Which of these theories are true? Well, in a shamanic and magical fashion, they are all true. There are those who would wish for their own pet theory to be the correct one, who think the truth is this but not that. But there is no reason to assume that one elf is right and some other is not. Everyone, if sHe is being true to hir own inner sense and mythology is correct for hir own s'elf. Some of us came here from the Seven Sisters, some of us from Sirius, other elfae from other stars, sometimes unnamed, as well. Where we all came from before that we can not know precisely except to say what is obvious, which is that we all came from the Divine Magic originally, which is the source of all things, and lives within each and every one of us. We are the starlight that formed the stars.

The idea that elves and elfae are star folk is an ancient idea, based upon the notion, in part, that we are the Eldar or Elder Race that came here before mankind arose and became, at least temporarily, the dominant and dominating force on this planet. However, there is also no reason to assume that there are not earth elves, as well as star elves. Elves who were born first and foremost upon the Earth and didn't have their spirits and souls migrate here from other star systems. We know at least a few of these.

Our sisters of the Elf Queen's Daughters used to talk about Oanians as well. These folk came from a planet in a distant star system that was predominately composed of water. This system produced many of the Selkies, Sea Sprites and Merfolk, and those who are of this race in humanoid bodies, tend to be natural swimmers. They not only love the water, but if thrown in any body of water, will float. Our daughter when she was about two and three years old would spend hours in the bathtub submerging hers'elf, until her skin looked like a raisin and she would reluctantly agree to get out.

There is a tendency due to the Tolkien effect, we might call it, or the fantasy effect, perhaps, to think that there is but one history and origin for our folk. But if that is so, as we say, it was so long past that none but the greatest seers, those who are expert in Paltareon, the Far Memory of the Elves, would be able to see it and then it would only lead them eventually to the Source, the Divine Magic. From there we, like the stars thems'elves, spread out into the Universe, going in all directions and we are spreading out still. This fact and tendency may be in part why elves appear to be born all over the Earth and not just awakening in one specific place. We are star gypsies by our very natures and ever migrating and forever in the process of a mystical and magical peregrination, like the stars going out from and eventually back to the Source. And when we come together in the midst of these journeys, passing each other by or staying together for a time, it is a most wondrous thing. Love is shared and magic and luck abounds and Elfin is born in the center of our gathering, in the space between us, and the touch that we share.

"The Elven Way is not a religion or a cult. It could be described as a movement but it is probably best understood as a dance." ——Old Elven Saying

Who came first, elves or faeries?

This is a little bit like the chicken or the egg dilemma. However, most people these days conceive of faeries as being small humanoid beings with the wings of butterflies, dragonflies or moths for the most part and this conception of faeries comes primarily from Victorian times (see *The Dragon Legacy* by Nicholas De Vere and *Realm of the Ring Lords* by Laurence Gardner). (Also note that we are not saying that there are no winged-beings of any kind, including the Deva Realm, but that the idea of faeries as tiny creatures is not an ancient concept.) This notion of tiny humanoid winged faeries is a very recent one. In that sense, elves did very much come first. And this is so at least as far as the fact that the general conception of elves, which these days is mostly derived from Tolkien, is closer to the traditional understanding of the Elven and Faerie folk, the combination of which these elves refer to as elfin or elfae. This is not to say that elves came before faeries or faeries before elves, but that the modern conception of elves is much more ancient than the notion that is currently popular concerning faerie folk.

The truth is that elves, faeries, pixies, brownies, the Sidhe and various other forms of faerie elfin folk are all merely various tribal formations, bands and groups of one essential people. Asking if the elves or faeries came first is like asking if First Nation tribes of the Sioux or the Cheyenne came first. Or the Apaches or the Navajos came first. We are all related peoples.

It is interesting to us, however, that the conception of faeries as winged little humans is so popular. This is truly a relatively recent innovation on faerie lore, created according to some folks to diminish the significance of our peoples, and it has little support in ancient lore except in the fact that the dwarves are often conceived of as being short of stature. Still, this idea has taken root in the minds and hearts of many folk so strongly that there are those who speak with these little winged ethereal beings. Which means, in effect, that this thought form is so powerful that such beings have actually been created on the astral and etheric realms of being, with some manifestation, mostly in an etheric fashion, according to these seers, on the material plane.

For our own part, these elves see the butterflies, dragonflies and moths as being these faeries. We don't demand that they be anthropomorphized beings, giving them human bodies in order to see them as people but accept them for the unique faeries beings that they truly are. We also embrace many trees as being elfin in nature and many birds as well.

Now, we don't have a problem with those who envision faeries as little winged human beings, except for the fact that these are often the folks who insist on faeries being in that form and deny our existence as living and manifest elves. And they often also fail to see or relate to modern manifest faerie folk who often wear various forms of faerie wings or elf ears in order to feel more truly our own s'elves as well as announce to the world our own unique faerie natures.

We would remind these folks that the idea of faeries as small, winged humanoids is a fairly modern idea and that the idea that the elves and faerie folk exist as manifest human beings interacting with mankind and others is nearly as ancient as the elfin ours'elves are. But being tolerant folk, we are perfectly happy with their conception of the fae as long as they don't deny our own true existence. (See our books the *Elven Way* and *Liber Aelph*).

~

Is it the Elf Star or the Faerie Star? And who first adopted the seven-pointed star as the Elf Star and what does it mean?

Really, it is both. We call the seven-pointed acute-angled star the "Elven Star" because it was our sisters of the Elf Queen's Daughters, EQD, (of which Zardoa was a member in their Carbondale. Il., vortex/coven) who in the 70s first adopted and started using this star to represent the elves in the letters they wrote and circulated to elfin folk (see our Silver Elves books *Elf Magic Mail*, volumes one and two, in which we have reproduced the original contents of those letters and described the graphics that adorned them and have also added our commentary about the letters and the sisterhood.) Our sisters Arwen and Elanor first conceived (in this lifetime) of using this star for the elven and put them upon the EQD letters on numerous occasions. Since the five-pointed star represented Mankind (inspired in Arwen's mind by Da Vinci's Vitruvian Man), Arwen Eveningstar added wings to that figure (so one ray for the head, two for the arms, two for the legs, and two for the wings) and thus came up with a seven-pointed star to represent the Elves and the evolution of humankind into the Angelic Realms. Obviously, due to the wings, it represents our faerie kindred as well. In fact, the very first letter of the *Elf Magic Mail* that had this symbol showed a five-pointed star with wings called the "Winged Star." Thus from the very beginning of its adoption as the Elven Star, the idea existed beneath the surface that this was also the Faerie Star. So it represents all Fae folk, elves, pixies, faeries, brownies and others and all are welcome to use it.

We Silver Elves have, for our own part, worn the elven star as an amulet for over 40 years. We have at least a half dozen variations of it. From a very small elf star less than an half inch from side-to-side that we have upon one of our magical elven wands that we created, to a necklace piece that was made for us individually and is about three & a half inches in diameter. We even have one, about two inches across that comes from Jerusalem. We also have one that our sister Loriel gave us as a birthday gift that is a seven-pointed flower. And Arwen, Elanor, and Loriel had a house south of Half Moon Bay that had a huge seven-pointed elf star, about six or seven feet in diameter, that was painted on the side of their home. We lived with them for over a month in the late 1970's at this somewhat Rivendell like abode.

For our own part, we carried on the tradition, putting it on our own *The Magical Elven Love Letters* (see volumes one, two and three) throughout the 80s and 90s that we sent out to our elven and otherkin kin and over the years it apparently caught on. It would be nice, to our minds, if our kindred knew where it came from, the story of its first adoption as the Elven Star by the EQD, as it is part of modern elven and faerie history. But in the long run, it doesn't really matter. What does matter is that this star speaks to the heart of the elfae (the elven and faerie folk) and it is this reason that it has been taken up and carried on and used again and again to represent us.

And surely, this would not have happened if in fact the elven/faerie star didn't have something ancient to it. It sings to our hearts and imaginations because it truly connects us to our ancient kindred and it resonates in our Collective Unconscious. Otherwise it would have gone the way of so many things that have been put out there but passed by and forgotten. It calls to us. It reminds us of who we truly are and that is what truly matters. For it is the Elven-Faerie Star and we are all the kindred that it shines upon.

༺

Are the legends true that say elves kidnap people?

Most of the ancient lore about the elven and fae have stories of us kidnapping people, exchanging their babies for ours, or capturing or enchanting them when they wander into Elfin and not allowing them to leave. This is, for the most part, nonsense but the part about enchanting people does have truth to it. It should be noted that we elves don't force people to stay in our realms, it's just that having eaten of our food or drunk of our waters or wine or even coffee or tea, which is to say having experienced our hospitality, they are not always eager to go. We nurture them when nearly everyone else wishes merely to criticize, argue or tell them what they think they should do and how they should live their lives, which in the opinion of those folks has been wrong up to that point.

It is true that sometimes we have to tell them we have things to do and show them to the door, telling them we love them, and of course that they can come back, but on another day. Otherwise they would just babble on and on about their difficulties with this or that person and we'd never get anything done.

Our sisters of the Elf Queen's Daughters, on the other hand, would often put them to work. Or send them on an adventure that would challenge their spirits and souls and prove enlightening for them. But we are less directive as individuals. We listen. We sympathize. If asked, we will offer advice, which is seldom heeded or followed despite being requested, on how to proceed. But mostly we trust in those who come to us to take charge of their own lives, although there are surely many who would rather we did so for them.

Did our ancestors ever kidnap people? Well, it's possible. Back in the days when we were being invaded by more aggressive peoples taking over our lands, enslaving us, massacring our people, we surely did many things to attempt to ensure the survival of our people, including exchanging our sweet babes with their own troll like grunting things, so that we could be raised among them. But those days are long past. We used our magic, along with their own fervent wishes to convince them that we didn't really exist (for you don't go around looking to kill people who don't exist) and we learned, at the same time, the magic of incarnating in any body we so choose and thus, after our culture was decimated, we choose to be born among them, secreting our elven magic and culture deep within our souls.

Now we have no need to kidnap them and take them to Elfin and honestly, they wouldn't appreciate it if we did. By which we mean, not only would they not like being treated the way they tend to treat others, but they just don't for the most part have the spiritual development and maturity of soul to appreciate the wonders of Elfin. Where we see magic, they see the dull interior of their own souls and the empty reflections of their imaginations.

Why would we even wish such people in Elfin? If we could actually heal them... heal their souls and their spirits ... that would make a great difference but alas, without their willingness to be healed we cannot do so. As much as we'd like and truly desire to share our wondrous realm with everyone who desires to enter it, the fact is that most folks are simply not ready for such revelations. And in many ways, the passage into Elfin must be earned by the development of the individual spirit or they just pass out again as quickly as they entered. In that sense, the entrance into Elfin is a revolving door. Until you understand how to get off, you just end up where you started from, or go endlessly in circles.

It is true that in the past there have been times when individuals have wandered into our realms and imbibed this or that substance that suddenly made it possible for them to be able to see what they hadn't been able to previously. But such wonders, such awakenings usually only last for about a year in our experience and if the person doesn't have something truly fae in hir, sHe fades back into the world. Yet still, such individuals find their way in the long run to the realms for which they are destined and we ever bless them upon their way. For few are actually meant to stay with us, except for a short while, for most we are but a place of rest and healing upon their journey. A sojourn of acceptance and gentle kindness, a temporary sanctuary for most, except those very few who are truly destined to realize they are our very own.

☙

What will happen to us if humanity destroys itself?

*E*lves know ours'elves to be essentially spirit beings. We are not elves because of the shape of our bodies but rather our bodies are manifestations of our spirit. If it should happen, and we truly hope it doesn't for it would be inconvenient for us, that man and some other kind destroy the environment to the point where we are unable to live upon the Earth in humanoid form, we would, of course, find other forms or planetary systems to live within and upon.

The vast majority of unawakened humans would in those circumstances reincarnate in whatever animal, fish or insect forms might be available and begin again the slow evolutionary ascent. Some elfin folk would go to other planets where similar forms might be found and some few, truly evolved elfin would rise to take their place among the Shining Ones.

It is also possible and perhaps in a way likely that some elfin would simply bide their time, living on the astral planes in the sort of nether and ethereal realms of Elfin that many folks assume to be the true Elfland, waiting for circumstances to develop where we may proceed with our efforts to master our ability to manifest upon the material planes of existence. Stepping from this to another timeline, another parallel world.

But our great hope is that enough of humanity will wake up and, even now in what seems to be this late date, transform thems'elves sufficiently to continue our evolution upon this most wondrous crystal blue planet.

༒

Are elves the people of the future?

We elves often think of ours'elves as an advanced race, and by this we mean a spiritual race of beings. We often refer to ours'elves as the People of the Dawning Age, the People of the Ancient Future and so on, advancing the idea that as humanity evolves it will generally become more elfin in nature. In much the same fashion that ape-like beings evolved into men, we frequently are of the opinion that men and others will evolve into elfae of various sorts. This is not an uncommon notion really. Mankind holds it as well. Thus there are numerous books, graphic novels and movies about mutants, futants, x-men, and other humans that have acquired various powers and abilities.

And there is surely truth to this concept for certainly humanity will evolve, diversify further, branching out into sub-species, and if it is to survive become more capable of doing so. It would be erroneous, however, if we were to suppose that everyone will become an elf or a fae folk of some sort. Each race of being, each individual, will evolve in their own way. We elfae surely will also evolve, becoming more of what we already are in potential and we can expect that other races will develop as well, or, if not, possibly pass from existence.

The notion that this evolution will take place primarily in the form of the attainment of superpowers of the martial sort is both possible and, at the same time, unlikely. This idea stems from the basic tendency here in the Kali Yuga, or most material of ages, to conceive of everything in reference to the material world. But such superpowers are really little different in their way, for the most part, from guns and other advanced technology. Will technology advance further in the future? Surely it will. Will we develop superpowers? Quite possibly so. But if superpowers are just another means of fighting and killing each other, we will not have really evolved at all. We will have merely strengthened our means of engaging in conflict with each other.

The real evolution toward advanced elven being won't be about gaining superpowers and abilities but about becoming more tolerant as spiritual beings and at the same time more capable of cooperation. We will cherish, nurture and empower individuality while increasing our capacity to love each other, rid ours'elves of prejudice, and work toward common goals, as well as just learning to get out of the way of others, not involve ours'elves in and have opinions about things that don't really concern us and generally apply the principle of live and let live and the manifestation of the Golden Rule, do unto others, to life overall.

In that way, humanity *will* be becoming more elfin. Not necessarily elfin in the way that they imagine us, which is rather like them only with magical powers, but as people who are truly able to love each other and foster the good in all beings. The superpowers we will develop won't so much be the powers of waging war but of healing, nurturing and advancing our creative abilities on all planes and levels.

It is not that we won't have need of protecting ours'elves. As elves, we are long accustomed to having to use various arts of camouflage and other skills to securing our s'elves and our others. But our greatest weapons, when weapons are absolutely called for, have ever been our superior intelligence, our willingness to compromise and our essentially loving dispositions combined with our enchanting personalities. As we truly develop these to their fullest, we will have no real need to defend ours'elves because others will submit to us of their own accord knowing to the depth of their souls that we will inevitably do what is best for each and everyone.

"Some people say the path to elfin is winding and crooked, but that is usually because many of those who tread it are confused and uncertain at first. Elves are great proponents of the path of least resistance and seek the easiest way to do nearly everything. Thus the road to Faerie is simple. One needs but be true to one's own fae nature and all else follows therefrom."

—*Wisdom of the Eldars*

Chapter 7:
How Elves Relate to Other People

> Once an elf finds hir identity as an elf, sHe will often begin to search for other elves, even look for a community of elven. We have had a number of sisters and brothers new on the Elven Path to disclose to us that they had a great struggle both finding other elves to relate to and relating in general to other people, both normal people and Otherkin. We are often asked for tips on doing so, and as we try in this chapter to answer some of the questions about this dilemma of relationships with others, we cover some of the ways we have dealt with our own struggles in this world with relationships.

Why are elves born into the normal world?

Some may wonder why we elves are born into the families of normal folk, often among the more or less normal folk, and particularly scattered here and there throughout the world. In other words, why aren't we born all together in one place? And the answer is, as is so often the case with the elves, complicated.

One of the most obvious reasons is because the normal folk (which is to say the folk that call themselves normal and ever wish to be normal, doing everything they can to conform and appear normal) pretty much dominate the world by sheer numbers. There are more of them than us and we have survived as a race (and we are defining elven as a 'spiritual race') mainly by hiding/camouflaging ours'elves among them.

While it may seem that we elves are born to normal folk, choosing to incarnate among them, because, well, we have little choice, there are things we can learn about the world by studying them. At the same time, in many ways the reality is that while it may seem that we are born among the normal folk, we are most often born among those elfae who are really pretending, quite expertly at times, we admit, to be normal. One or both of our parents may actually seem somewhat normal but are really "passing" in the world of man. There is almost always at least one very unusual and eccentric individual in our upbringing, besides ours'elves of course (see *The Soul's Code* by James Hillman) that influences us greatly.

There is, however, another reason that we are born among the normal folk, which is also an aspect of survival for our people and that is: our exposure to them and their ways, serves as a sort of inoculation for us. Once having had a thorough doze of normal humanity, the vast of majority of we elfae are never in danger again of coming down with normalcy, which can be a life stifling spiritual disease, eventually resulting in people walking around like zombies, spouting inane opinions and arguing about nearly everything and endlessly concerned with petty and insignificant things. It is not so much that normalcy takes your breath away, as enchantment will tend to do, but rather it sucks the life out of you, whereas enchantment fills you with life. (See our book *The Keys of Elfin Enchantment*.)

So then, why are we born so far apart from each other? Often seeking most of our lives just to find our true kindred and often making do with whomever we find. And again, the answer is varied. First of all, since most elfae have advanced to the point where we can have some say in the body we will inhabit, the parents who raise us and the environment we wish to be born within, we choose those things among these possibilities that best suit our own spiritual quest or our mission in a particular lifetime. We are not merely here to seek and hang out with each other. If that was the case, most of us would just remain in Elfin and never interact with other folk at all. We are here to develop our spirits and souls, enhance our magical abilities and to accomplish certain things, most of all the establishment of Elfin upon the Earth.

It is important to consider that we, ours'elves, are infectious with elven magic and healing. Everyone that comes into contact with us is changed in subtle ways, mostly by having whatever part of each individual that is of Faerie or Elfin stirred a bit. We are a mystery to them and we arouse wonder, even when it is only a very minor or simple wonder, a wonder that makes people curious, a wonder that peeks their interest and makes them muse and imagine for a moment.

Of course, one might ask, if we are born so far apart from each other usually, and there is a purpose to this being so, why then do we spend so much time seeking to connect with each other. And the answer is, being elves how could we not hunger to be together? However, it is also important to understand that we are, each and every one of us, little radio stations broadcasting out our elven magical energy.

As we grow more adept, obtain mastery, and certainly as we gather together, our range of influence becomes stronger and wider and our broadcast is picked up by other elven stations/folk who pass it along, adding their own twist and style to the mix that is our culture. These elven broadcasts develop into sort of leylines, or as our aboriginal cousins of Australia would call them, Songlines, which is an idea we elves particularly love. These interconnected Songlines then radiate out into the world, transforming all who are open to the Song of Elfin, and consequently elven magic, like wildflowers, begins to spring up everywhere.

❦

What say the elves about living in the world of the unawakened?

It often seems to the elven, and this is not without a good deal of justification, that one lives in a world surround by what are variously called the unenlightened, the unawakened, the muggles (a la Harry Potter), the mundane or the normal folk (so called because that is how they like to think of themselves). But from an elven point of view, the whole world is full of magic and nearly everyone, with very few exceptions, are magicians of various sorts, although most don't acknowledge that fact, or conceive things in that way.

This means that we are also surrounded by people who may call themselves men or woman but who are, in most cases, some variety of fae folk. They are orcs or goblins, grimlens, hobbits, pixies, brownies, faeries, elves and all manner of otherkin and hobs (halflings) of various kinds. Most, of course, don't think of themselves in this way, which is in fact the point. They are unawakened to their true natures. But even if they are unaware of who they are, we usually get some sense of their real being and may guide them, gently, toward that realization. In doing so, we must be careful of not forcing our own opinions and aspirations upon them. Our task is to guide them to their own realization. It is not our place to slap them awake (as much as that may seem necessary or justified) but to awaken them gently with the song of Elfin.

☙

Do you tell all people you meet that you are elves?

Sometimes. It really depends upon the person. Most folks in the world don't know what to do with such a revelation. They don't believe in elves and faeries and others in the first place so telling them we are elves is really, in most cases, a waste of time and merely opens us up to ridicule and scorn. Even those who believe in faeries as etheric or astral beings, don't always accept that we are elves manifest in human bodies. They can accept the one idea of beings that are invisible to most others (but usually not to them) but find the idea that we might choose to incarnate in human form too much to embrace. Why they would wish to limit their perceptions, understanding and intelligence in this way, we are uncertain. However, we accept that there are certain individuals (quite a few actually) who are not ready to enter the deeper realms of Elfin, or simply to acknowledge that it exists at all.

The question then becomes: how do you determine who is or isn't ready for or open to the realization that we elves do exist in physical form. Well, beside the fact that it is simply clear in many cases, there are a large number of people for whom the answer is ambiguous. In order to gauge a person's reaction to our actual existence as elves in this world, these elves approach this dilemma lightly, often presenting individuals with a sort of test of their own degree of openness, understanding and degree of development in a playful way.

Sometimes we simply say, when an opening in conversation allows, "We're elves," and then see how they react. Often individuals just laugh and we laugh along with them, as though we are kidding. But sometimes someone will say, "Oh, I'm an elf, too," or "I'm a dwarf," or "I'm a faerie," or whatever. Then we know that we have a kindred of some sort who is willing, at least to a certain degree, to play along with us as we dance closer and closer to Elfin, drawing them deeper into the elvish realms.

At times, we will tell someone our elven names and when they ask what sort of names they are, thinking we might say, Polish or Romanian or whatever, we reply, "Elven." This, of course, tends to produce the same variety of reactions that directly telling them we are elves, does.

Of course, some folks think that we are just kidding. They assume we are cosplayers, or *Dungeons and Dragons* players or some other sort fantasizing about being elves and we are content to let them believe whatever they will. We elves, particularly we Seelie folk, don't tend, for the most part, to lie to people unless absolutely necessary to protect ours'elves and our people. We simply let them deceive their own selves. And, honestly, they are quite eager to do so. We could try to tell them the truth but really, they don't want to know the truth and can't and won't accept it, anyway. So why should we bother? We have no real vested interest in them believing we are elves.

In that way, we are truly a kind of secret or esoteric society. Only other elves and fae really know and understand that we are elven. And really, that's probably for the best.

☙

Where do you find kindred fae?

Certainly the question we get asked the most, usually by those who are newly exploring their elven nature, is where to find one's kindred elfae and how to connect with them. Alas, while we say, and quite accurately, that this is a question most asked by the newly awakened, it is unfortunately a problem that confronts most elves no matter how long they have been awakened or how evolved as elfin they may be. The only difference is that those who have been awakened for a good deal of time have usually found one or two elves that they can associate with regularly, although the difficulty with finding new kindred remains the same.

The fact is that in this day and age elves are few and far between. Going to faerie and elf fests or pagan festivals (for those who can do that and many of us cannot afford to do this or do it very often) is a means for connecting with others of our kind; the smaller the festival, in fact, in most cases, the better. And social media is another way to connect, but for these elves most of our relationships have come via destiny and our own elf work, which is to say the creative activity, in our case writing The Magical Elven Love Letters and other of our books and sharing them as much as we are able. Thus our advice to those seeking other elves or fae is to create some form of elven art/writing/music and share it as widely as possible.

~

How does an elf find friends?

Most elves, by our natures, are enchanters and surely enchantment is the most elven of the magical arts, which doesn't mean that we don't explore or study or use other of the Arts Magical but that enchantment is what we are historically most associated with and is the magic that is most in keeping with our own dispositions in the majority of cases. And as enchanters, ever seek to be friends/elf friends with everyone we encounter, although, it is true that not everyone is open to this, and certainly most are not immediately open. In that sense, we are like the ocean slowly weaving down cliffs of their suspicion and reluctance or like ivy we grow on people.

Because of this and because of our elf sight, our ability (Verfaji see our book *Arvyndase*) not only to see magic that others do not see but also to see an indication of who is elvish and what their elvish nature may be, we relate to people based not only on who they are but who they are destined to be. We relate to their potential, ever seeking to nurture the best that is in them. Thus we make friends with all sorts of folks, although we, like most elven, wish there were more folks who were aware and awakened to the point that they could share this path with us with the same relish we do. Still, we find gnomes and faeries, pixies, leprechauns and all manner of other folk and even if they are not entirely aware of their own natures, we have some inner spiritual understanding of what they may become. We interact with them as they are, without making any demands upon them to be otherwise, while nurturing what they will in time surely become.

☙

How do you deal with individuals who pretend they are more spiritually evolved or more magically adept than they really are?

We have been asked a number of times by our elven kin: How do we deal with individuals who pretend they are more spiritually evolved or more magically adept than they really are? Our answer is always the same: "kindness served with a bit of healing magic and compassion."

We are initiates of a number of guru groups and meditation systems and in those groups individuals were frequently told to give up their egos and their egoic projections. In fact, we use to know this family of Otherkin whose Thane was a very charismatic individual and would often and easily draw people to her. However, whenever anyone came and proceeded to brag of how evolved sHe (she/he) was and how sHe was going to do this or that to transform the world (almost overnight), this Thane and her fellow family members would ridicule the individual and basically quite thoroughly humiliate hir (him/her). We elves actually felt quite sorry for these individuals. It is true that they were boasting and making quite a bit more of them selves than they truly deserved or had earned but we were not certain that they merited getting such comeuppance, and we doubted that it did little to actually help them evolve as individuals.

Not too long ago, we were in the laundry room doing our wash when a woman who lives in the same building as we came in and started telling us how, many years ago, she had taken a seminar in Reiki and how she had undergone all three initiations within a day and how everyone was amazed at how evolved she was. We listened to this with a smile. We were certain that even if she did take all three initiations in a day that she had never done a thing with Reiki since that day and that she was merely endeavoring to make us believe she was far more evolved than she truly was and we were not fooled (certainly, a truly highly evolved person would not be boasting about it, and certainly not in a laundry room). But neither were we offended by this. We asked ours'elves, why would she be bothering to tell us this in the first place? Why would she be seeking to make us think she was some highly evolved spiritual being? And we came to the conclusion that she did so because that's what she thought we were. She wanted to impress us because she thought we are important people and she desired to look good in our eyes. So, as we said, we smiled and nodded and congratulated her on her success and acted very impressed, all while silently giving her an elven blessing. For our goal is ever to encourage individuals toward enlightenment and while she may not be as evolved as much as she pretended to be, we are also surely far less evolved than she supposed. Her bragging about herself was actually a compliment to us and we found we could but encourage her on path.

Silver Flame on the edge of the Redwood Forest begins a ritual of Elven Blessings as a healing magic of love and compassion.

Do elves hate dwarves?

Some people get the idea from reading Tolkien and viewing *The Hobbit* and *Lord of the Rings* movies that there is some eternal conflict between elves and dwarves. This is not entirely dissimilar to the idea that some people have that cats and dogs are eternally in conflict. But the truth is cats can get along with dogs and vice versa and cats may fight with cats or dogs with dogs. There is nothing that necessitates that elves and dwarves have to be in competition and conflict. It is a convenient dramatic aspect for fiction but it is not really a fact of reality. Elves are not inclined to hate anyone actually.

However, it should be noted that the conflict between the elves and dwarves in Tolkien's works is based primarily on two factors and that is that the dwarves cut down the trees merely for their own convenience and that they care more for jewels and riches than for the mountains where they find them. In other words, in Tolkien's world dwarves tend to put material value and wealth above the beauty and preservation of Nature. And in as far as that goes, it would be true that we elves love the trees and hate to see them unnecessarily cut down. We mourn the loss of the forest and jungles and we weep to see the mountains torn down to provide wealth for those who are already wealthy and to provide energy that can be provided in other and less destructive ways.

In as far as any particular dwarf or orc or goblin or any other being destroys the environment merely for profit and fights the development of renewable resources then, yes, most elves would be in conflict with them. Not necessarily actively, but we surely disagree with their activities and their motives. But it is not them as individuals really that we are in conflict with but the ignorance that propels them to do such things. Still, we must admit that they also tend to ignore reason, ignore facts, deny science, promoting what they call alternate facts, and simply refuse to consider that what they are doing is destructive to the Earth and eventually to all of us upon it. And those things, such obstinate and determined greed, we are ever in conflict with.

☙

So if elves are born elven, are orcs born to be orcs as well?

We must say that the answer to this question is both yes and no. If we consider orcs, goblins and grimlens from the point of view that is expressed in so many stories that these individuals often seek to foster wickedness in the world, then we'd have to say no, they were not born to do so. Rather they are raised or reared (and we do mean reared and beaten) to do so. Just as abusers have often been abused as individuals, so do some individuals become orc-like, or goblin-like, or grimlen-like because of the abuse they're suffered or the way they have been reared/abused.

Certainly, this was Tolkien's opinion when he stated that orcs were elves that had been tortured until they became orcs. And surely and unfortunately this is the fate of far too many innocent children who would grow up to be quite lovely and loving (elfin) beings if it weren't for the fact that they are brutalized by their parents or others, by the often cruel way of the world as some folks have created it and insist upon it being.

They are raised by those who are always trying to toughen them up for the harsh world they will encounter as they grow up.

And surely there is some karmic link or lesson that is involved with this as well. We choose our incarnation, although some individuals are so desperate to be reborn they don't bother to read the fine print, so to speak, of the body and life they choose. But what we need ask ours'elves is if orcs, grimlens and goblins have to be the cruel and wicked to be orcs and so forth. Do you have to be evil or part of a conspiracy to take over the world and force your beliefs on others to be a grimlen? Is there no positive outlet for the orc?

Can a person be a good person, and intelligent, educated and kind individual and still be an orc? Well, really that is for the orcs, goblins and grimlens to decide for their own selves. It is not our place as elves to define what it means to be an orc or any other kind of being. We are doing well in attempting to define our own s'elves and live up to those definitions. And we certainly are not inclined to allow others to decide for us what constitutes our elven nature. We elfin, for our part, believe in the possibility, even the inevitability of evolutionary development and trust that someday orcs, grimlens, goblins and other Unseelie will be our friends as well as being, as they are, our fae cousins. That is surely our hope for them and for the world.

"If you read fantasy book about us, one might get the idea that we elves hate orcs, goblins and others of their kind but we do not. We ever wish them healing, enlightenment and evolutionary development. In the meantime, however, we may have to fill them with arrows to let the light in."

Is it necessary that we elves be forever in conflict with orcs, goblins and grimlens?

The conflict between elves and orcs, goblins and grimlens is a staple of many faerie tales both modern and traditional. As well as conflicts between the Seelie Elves, the elves of light and the Unseelie Elves who are generally conceived of being of a darker (in character) variety. From the point of view of these elves, however, most orcs, goblins and grimlens are some of our Unseelie cousins.

But is conflict necessary? Do we have to be at odds with such individuals? And, of course, the answer is no, it is not necessary at all, and surely not what we elves of the Seelie races desire, for we would be friends with everyone who is really ready and willing to be true friends with us.

But let's look at what are some of the modern manifestations of these beings. If you want to find orcs, in many cases, you need look no farther than violent biker gangs cooking up and selling meth, guns and engaging in other illegal activities. This is not to say that all bikers are violent or engage in illegal activities, or that all bikers are orcs or that all orcs are bikers, but still if you are looking to see the modern manifestation of orcs then that's a good place to start. And ask yours'elf, do you like to be around such individuals? Would you like them as so-called friends? Or would you rather avoid them if at all possible?

And if you are looking for grimlens, then religious fanatics are usually full of them, particularly those of a violent variety. The Taliban, the members of Isis/Isil, Christians who bomb abortion clinics and kill doctors, are all, more than likely, of grimlen descent. These folks would be psychopaths, except they need permission to do what they really want to do, which is kill people, and they find that permission in their particular version of their religion. But really, they just want to kill as well as force their beliefs and rules for life on everyone else.

And this is not to say that all grimlens are killers or are religious fanatics. They are not. These elves used to know a grimlen who actually helped us out, but we knew we always had to be a bit careful around him and could never reveal any of our inner secrets to him.

And goblins, who we sometimes refer to as Greedies or Gobleers, because of the propensity to overeat and leer at those they desire sexually, can quite often be found in corporations as CEO's, as lawyers and certainly as politicians. They are generally, but not always, more intelligent than either the orcs or grimlens in our experience and often manipulate those individuals to their own ends.

But must we hate them? Must we be ever in conflict with them? We surely hope not. Our greatest wish for them is to see them evolve into more kind, compassionate and cooperative folk. But then, this is our wish for everyone.

"Every people have their wizards." — Old Elven Saying meaning don't let prejudice blind you to talent and appreciate the genius in everyone.

What do elves feel about transgender indiviuals?

We suppose it should be obvious that since we elven base our definitions of race more on character than physical characteristics that we are not really concerned, as some folks seem to be, with whether one is of this or that gender. This is particularly true since elves are often seen as being androgynous anyway and even when we are not homosexual or bisexual we still tend to have a certain bisexual vibe to us, at least in the eyes of the normal folk. Thus the notion that one is or should be restricted to the gender they were born with, or god given gender as they would put it, does not accord with our thinking or philosophies at all.

To us, having gender reassignment surgery is not really different than any other cosmetic surgery, or wearing a wig, or wearing make up or having your ears made more pointed or even going to the dentist and getting false teeth or having a crown put on. It is simply a matter of an attempt to adjust one's body to one's feelings and sense of s'elf and that is nearly always a good thing as far as the elves are concerned, particularly when one improves one's life by doing so.

These elves have known many individuals, mostly kindred of ours, who have had gender reassignment surgery so we are quite used to these beloved ones. In fact, one of the inner circle of the Elf Queen's Daughters had had that surgery, although years later she expressed to us the fact that, in many ways, it had turned to be, for her, more of a lark than a significant feeling event.

We remember sitting on one of the couches in the living room of the elven manor where she lived with us and about a half dozen other elves, some like us who tended to come and go over the years, when she suddenly pulled off her wig exposing her bald head. And she said, and now we are paraphrasing since it's been nearly forty years since that conversation and we know from experience that we are unlikely to remember it exactly, "I don't know why I got the change. I had to go to psychiatrists and tell them a bunch of bullshit that they wanted to hear, but none of it was true for me. I just thought that being a woman might be more powerful magically in this age, but in the meantime I've discovered that women can be just as crazy as men and sometimes even crazier." And she went on to say, "The only thing that really matters isn't gender but the development of one's spiritual nature, of becoming more elven or whatever one happens to be. The rest is just a bunch of buffoonery."

And this is the reality for the truly elven. We do not define our s'elves by our bodies and thus are not very gender oriented. We don't tend to have women's groups or men's groups the way grimlens, goblins and even mankind often do for while we are usually male or female or sometimes a bit of both, we are not and never have been men or women and gender is far less significant to us than the love we share for each other and our eternal kindreth in Elfin. Plus, we don't like to be separated from each other, particularly due to arbitrary barriers based on physical characteristics and the lunacy and prejudice of the unenlightened. We will always, if given the chance, choose to be together in our eternal elven frasority (combining the words for fraternity and sorority).

And when it comes to bathrooms, if it was up to most of us, they would all be unisex anyway. What do we care, we're just there to do our business and get it done so we can get back to the party or the magic at hand, and certainly to each other. Everything else is just doing the dishes as far as we are concerned.

We know that there are some folks who would argue with this because they want to cling to their past and drag their preconceptions into Elfin, but as long as they continue carrying that baggage around with them, desperately clutching those old mind sets, Elfin True will elude them. It is only when we have the magical strength and power to become anew, to truly give up our old ways of thinking and perceiving, will we find our way into Elfin deep and join with all our kindred there. And what a wondrous and joyous day that will be.

༼༽

Who are the Elf Friends?

Well, to resort to a bit of elven circle talk, our friends are our elf friends. The curious thing about Elf Friends is that this term can refer to both elves and others. One doesn't need to be an elf to be an elf friend, neither does one need to be other than elfin to be so. Consistent friendliness is the only true requirement.

As we have said in the last section, we've even had a grimlen as a friend, although we were very cautious in this friendship. Friendly, but circumspect. We've also had many rangers of various sorts as friends. They can be amazingly useful, particularly when it comes to dealing with the normal world in many ways. Not to mention the fact that they are often wizards at auto mechanics and various other mechanical things that, quite frankly, tend to confound these elves. Which is not to say that all elves are mechanically challenged, just that this is an area of expertise that we have yet to master, have very little real interest in, and would much prefer, when possible to have others deal with for us. Thus we are quite thankful for the rangers we have known and thankful that the magic has always brought them to us just when we needed them.

We've also had elf friends among dwarves, gnomes, brownies, pixies, faeries and all manner of folk. And like most folks we've had dogs who were elf friends, cats, trees, an iguana, a dragonfly and many other sorts of other.

Those who are our elf friends, or friends to the elves, are beloved by us. To be a true friend to the elves is to be considered a part of our family. We would even consider such folk as being elven or elfin, although in most cases they have not the slightest interest in such things. They are content being what they are, often obstinately so. They just happen to like us, are usually a bit intrigued by us and often do what they can to further us and aid us and we do the same for them.

Of course, as per the example of the grimlen that was an elf friend to us, one must be a bit careful at times in what one may reveal or how close one can let them into the inner family. But, really, that is true of nearly all families, isn't it. Frequently, one has uncles or cousins who, due to their prejudices, cannot be fully accepted into the inner circles of the family. You never know when they will go off on some illogical racist rant about faeries or brownies at family gatherings, but who are, none-the-less, fully accepted for who they truly are and are thus our elf friends, but not quite with all the benefits they might enjoy if they were more fully kin to us.

We love such as these. We accept them as they are, for they are impermeable to change and illumination, set in their ways, obstinate beyond reason, and yet, elf friends all the same and we do what we can for them, as they, in turn, do what they can for us. We may not, and surely are unlikely, to agree about politics, religion or what is acceptable social practice, but we do agree that we like each other to a certain extent and enjoy each other's company from time to time as well as being useful to each other. To such as these we are unlikely to ever reveal the inner secrets of our elven frasority but then they wouldn't understand them anyway.

So that brings us around again to who are the elf friends. Well, they are the friends to the elves. And in as much as they are true and loyal to us, we shall always be so to them and reward them as best we can with our love eternal and our aid when needed and in just such ways kindreth is born, nurtured and eventually matures into magical awareness.

"Elfin magic is subtle. No matter how things seem to be going it is ever moving us closer to Elfin. It's just that sometimes to get there we must travel through darkened valleys and shadowed forests. But have faith. In the end, we will emerge into the radiant light of Elfin and wonder why we ever doubted at all."

— *Wisdom from Elven Magicians*

Chapter 8:
Elven Lifestyle

> How elves live their daily lives is unique to each elf. We are an extremely varied people and when people ask us questions about elven lifestyle like "are elves vegetarian," we have to say it depends on the elf. When answering these questions, we try to mention the various possibilities of the lifestyle of our elven sisters and brothers, while sharing about our own preferences. In this chapter, we explore questions about our elven diet, our costumes, our celebrations, and how we govern our communities.

Are elves vegetarian?

We have addressed this question in a number of our books but because among elfin online groups this has been the most hotly debated and often, therefore, the most avoided and controversial topic, we think it bears speaking of again.

The simple answer, like so many things concerning elves, and as Tolkien pointed out so cleverly, is both yes and no. Some elves are vegetarian and some are not. These elves are mostly vegetarian, which means we don't usually eat meat, and almost never among ours'elves, but we do eat meat in limited quantities with others sometimes. It should be remembered that these elves were first awakened to our elven natures by the

Elf Queen's Daughters (EQD) in the mid 70s and manifested as a vortex of the sisterhood as the Elves of the Southern Woodlands. Thus our own magical training and development was greatly influenced by our sisters in the EQD. The sisters of the EQD used to say that the Law of Communion was higher than the Law of Dietary Restriction. This means that while we are essentially vegetarian, if someone offers us meat for dinner when we are their guests, we accept it (unless we had some medical reason not to do so). It would be rude not to do so and go against the all important uniting principle of community. On the other hand, we are rather liberal concerning others if they are our guests. If they desire meat when visiting us, we will fix it for them, although we are unlikely to imbibe ours'elves under such circumstances.

We choose to be vegetarian ours'elves because we seek to contribute as little unnecessary violence upon innocence animals as we can in the world. The world is already awash with violence and it really doesn't need more. But we are not the sort of people to enforce our beliefs upon others, or to say that all elves must be vegetarian. The most we will say about all elves is that all elves must make up their own minds on this and nearly every other subject.

We have known elves who have told us that they had to eat meat because their bodies required it, due to their blood type or whatever, or that they would die if they didn't consume meat. We suspect that such declarations are mostly spurious unless the person has a serious health condition, but we really don't care if it is true or not as we accept their own wishes for their choice of diet. As far as we are concerned, they could just say they like eating meat, or like the taste and smell of bacon (so do we, although we almost never eat it) and that would be okay with us. It is their decision and we are satisfied with leaving them to their own path and course of spiritual development and make no judgments about them for doing so. Elfin is enormous and there is surely room for all of us, although in our part of Elfin everything is magical and sacred and thus killing animals to eat just wouldn't seem right to us (not to mention that in Elfin, the deer are far too swift to catch even with an elven arrow). But we are each creating our own realms and others must do as their own hearts, imaginations and consciences dictate.

We have published an elven cookbook and while most of the recipes are vegetarian, we included a couple of recipes that offer an option for adding meat, especially for our meat eating otherkin. And if you are interested in trying some of our vegetarian dishes, *The Elf Folks' Book of Cookery: Recipes For a Delighted Tongue, a Healthy Body and a Magical Life* includes over 50 of our original dishes for all manner of faerie-elven folk like: Gypsie Potato and Mushroom Delight, Elven Minestrone Soup, Mermaid Navy Bean & Pine Nut Burgers, Wild Pixies Wild Rice Stuffed Peppers, and Dwarves Veggie Chili Soup. And be sure to try our Faerie Island Apple Pie with Fairy Tale Green Tea Almond Cookies.

"Elves will celebrate any holiday that involves merry making. However, if you are going to get serious and preach at us or subject us to solemn prayers, then there better be a free meal afterwards or we'll be slipping out the back door."

—— Knowledge of our Elven Life

What's the elfin view on wearing fur?

Those who are opposed to the wearing of fur and those who are strict vegetarian in our experience are often of the same disposition. And while we cannot speak for all elves, since no one can speak for all elves, we being, all of us, different and individual, these elves are against the slaughter of animals for their fur as we are, for the most part, against eating them when it is not necessary to do so. It just seems ignorant and wrong to us.

However, we understand that in the past and perhaps in some places in the present, one had to kill animals and wear their fur to survive in harsh conditions. But wearing it as a fashion statement in a world where one doesn't need to kill to live or need fur to stay warm is rather callous in our opinion and wears upon one's soul, making one less sensitive and aware.

Yet, like most things concerning elves, we make exceptions. While we don't buy fur to wear, we have to admit that no one as yet as far as we know has come up with a faux fur that is anywhere as cool as real fur is. And so sometimes these elves do wear fur, fur that we have obtained at flea markets and in *as is* stores, sometimes just left on the table at the end of the day and thrown away at a swap meet. Now, that really seems sacrilegious to us, to buy the fur of some poor animal raised for slaughter and then, when it was a little worn, or no longer in fashion, to just discard it. We feel a certain responsibility to honor these animals under these circumstances by wearing their fur. In many cases, we just hold onto the fur for years until we can incorporate it into some elfin costume we are making. We know that there will be those who will disagree with us for doing this and that is their privilege, just as they will disagree with the fact that we will eat meat if our host offers it to us.

Dr. Timothy Leary observed that in the years he spent living in the commune at Millbrook, the only violence that ever occurred was when some vegetarians beat up a guy for cooking a steak. We, for our own part, haven't seen vegetarians beating anyone up for eating meat, but we did have this friend on Facebook, who un-friended us because we posted a photo of some pagan musical group wearing fur. It could have been faux fur as far as we know. It was hard to tell from a photo on the internet. But this individual got totally angry with us for posting it. It wasn't even us wearing fur. (Eventually, after a few months, this individual requested to be our friend again, and of course, we were happy to allow this.) But to the minds of these elves, fanaticism is an even greater problem in the world than the unnecessary killing of animals for food or fur. We can understand how some folks wish to be very strict about these things for their own s'elves, but a certain tolerance for others seems in order. Otherwise, how can we have any influence on others who disagree with us if we don't at least try to understand their point of view, even if it doesn't always make sense? The fact is, you can't force people to change, at least not in any positive fashion.

There are those following Ancient Wisdom Traditions who proclaim that mankind is still working out their overall fear of animals left over from ancient days when they were dragged out of their dwellings and eaten by wild animals. It is thought that mankind will one day relax this inner fear that separates them from the animal kingdom and live more harmoniously with all animals; and at that point, meat eating will be a thing of the past. From an elven point of view this makes sense as we know humanity is evolving toward elfinness and this takes time. We elfin are beings of starlight and we believe that in our most evolved s'elves we are most nourished feeding off light.

⁂

What do the Silver Elves think of people who wear fake wings to be like faeries?

First, let us say. "We love it." We think people going around wearing faerie wings is wonderful. We are delighted every time that we encounter this phenomena. We also love it when individuals go about dressed as wizards or witches or whatever pleases and tickles their fancy. These elves do a variation of this, what we might call nouveau magic or elfin attire, which is wearing magical attire adapted to modern styles and vice versa.

To us, wearing faery wings about is not much different than someone wearing the traditional dress of their particular people and culture. These individuals are declaring their attachment to their culture and honoring it thereby. So, too, those who wear faerie wings are merely declaring to the world their faerie nature.

We are aware that certain individuals who are seen as authorities in the field of Fairy Faith lore hold the opinion that wearing faerie wings is a bit frivolous and doesn't take seriously the profound nature of our relationship with the Faerie Realms.

We disagree. We, on the other hand, don't present ours'elves as authorities in this field. We are elves and our opinion is from the point of view of these elves, and not necessarily all elves, but it seems to us that interacting with our realms with the seriousness that most folks hold while going to church (or pretend they are feeling), while surely a respectful thing to do, is not entirely necessary or even to be desired when relating to the realms of Faerie and Elfin.

While, like all people, we appreciate being treated with courtesy and respect (and in fact those who don't do so often have cause to regret it), we do not see ours'elves in such a serious light that we expect or demand that people treat us like holy people. In as much as people can be holy, we are no more or less holy potentially than anyone else. And for us, one of the things that we've noticed about those individuals that we consider to be holy, is their compassion and their sense of humor.

As far as we are concerned those who wear their faerie wings out and about are not being frivolous but being quite courageous. And we elves, like almost all people, greatly admire courage. We often wish that we were as courageous as they are. They inspire us and we are encouraged by them.

"Some people believe that true love is a fairy tale. It is, indeed. It is one of the greatest faerie magics ever created and we elves strive to manifest it every day."

— Ancient Elven Knowledge

What do the Silver Elves think of those who wear fake elf ears?

Like those who wear fairy wings in public, we are quite enchanted and a little bit in awe of those who wear elf ears out in public as well. Because we love photos of elves with elf ears, we adore the fact that there are those who have the courage to make their elfin natures known for all to see.

Of course, they will be seen as frivolous by some folks, and crazy by others, and surely immature by those who are caught up in the world and are eager to be taken seriously by conformist society, but that just makes their daring all the more wondrous to these elves. We wish we had the courage to do this ours'elves more often. We also wish we had a decent pair of elf ears, which we don't at this point, and were experts in makeup, which we also are not for we have noticed that some folks wear elf ears that are only minimally attached and don't really blend in with their actual ears and think that they could use a little makeup help as well. But then, at least they have the daring to wear the ears, and that, in itself, gains them our respect.

To us wearing elf ears, like wearing faerie wings, is the same as Native Americans wearing feathers or buckskin or whatever traditional costume their ancestors wore. They are paying respect in that way to their ancestors and while it is not necessary for them to do so, they are no less Native American for dressing in a suit and tie, and not necessarily less respectful concerning their ancestors. It is still nice sometimes, to remind ones'elf and others, who you really are.

So wear your elf ears, beloved kindred, and perhaps by your inspiration others will find the courage to do so as well.

~

Are there specific elfin holidays that the Silver Elves celebrate?

These elves don't have particular elven holidays that we celebrate, although there are other elves who do, either following the seasonal holidays of the pagan folk or following the seasonal celebrations that Tolkien outlined for the elven in his works (such as the elves of Tië eldaliéva, as the Elven Spiritual Path do). And surely there is great magic in doing so.

These elves, the Silver Elves, follow the Elven Way and are certainly not a religion nor do we follow any particular religion (although Elves in general are a varied people and many choose to also follow a religion of one kind or another, even invent new ones within a more Elven Faith or New Age Faith). One might observe that we are "elven wilde" or "elven free," and, for our part, celebrate nearly everything that involves delicious and free food, drink, presents and/or a good time. We do birthdays, Yule (have we mentioned that we love the great Elf Santa) and Halloween and usually Lupercolia (we also love our brother Pan). Our elven custom for celebrating birthdays is that one gets to celebrate their birthday a day for each year they are old. So this makes getting older such a pleasure and if you have enough people in your elven family, then you will be celebrating someone's birthday all year around.

We also do national holidays for our nation or someone else's nation, particularly Independence Days for our sisters and brothers of any free nation. And if they happen to be visiting us at that time, we will certainly celebrate any national holiday of their country that they wish. In fact, we even love to celebrate people coming to visit us. We will even help people celebrate their religious holidays as long as they don't involve us fasting, beating ours'Elves with sticks or going around looking somber pretending to be religious and spiritual. Generally, the only time we celebrate with people like that is when they go away. We are also known to celebrate the New Year a number of times each year according to the Gregorian calendar, and also according to South and Southeast Asian calendars.

However, we Silver Elves are fairly eclectic and improvisational folk. We celebrate when the opportunity presents itself. And many of our celebrations come spontaneously as a result of the completion of some elf project or creative work or of an impromptu gathering of elf kin or of around a natural phenomenon. Once a full moon magical circle we had turned into a week long healing gathering and celebration of elven spirits during an unexpected natural flood that kept us housebound for seven days. And while many of our elven celebrations are impromptu, at the same time we know that there are other elves who may wish for a bit more structure on their path. What we say is think for yours'Elf and create your own way, which works well for us; but others, particularly those who are beginning on the path and struggling to emerge from the pressure to conform to traditional society, may need or certainly desire a little more structure than we provide. And we understand that. We just don't have that structure to offer (although we do give suggestions for magical rituals and ceremonies in many of our books on The Elven Way including The Book of Elven Magick, Book 1 & 2). Stability, yes we do offer, for we are wilde spirited elves who have been around and with you in this lifetime for decades and will surely be here for you in many more lifetimes to come. But structure is just not in our elven nature. We provide inspiration for creativity. The creation of structure, we leave to other of our kindred.

༷

How do elven communities govern themselves? Do they have kings and queens?

Traditionally, elves are viewed in stories as having kings and queens, and this is the case even in modern stories, including urban fantasies about elves and fae folk. The reason for this is primarily, we believe, because most folks that wrote about us in the past were not elven and imagined our world was just a more magical version of their own world. They lived in kingdoms or queendoms and imagined that we did the same.

More modern writers tend to base their stories about us upon the tales of the past. They take ancient lore and rework it, although in some cases they just put a new mask upon it, and so accept the idea that our communities are a form of monarchy because that's what traditional lore says. And surely there is no great harm in this and it is perfectly understandable.

It is not easy to imagine what an elven form of government really is like, particularly when you are basing it upon the world around you. You, dear sisters and brothers, may wish to check out our book *The United States of Elfin: Imagining a More Elven Style of Government* to see our more elaborate thoughts on this matter.

Certainly, these elves, having been raised in a democracy are more inclined toward that form of government, a republic, really, but there is surely no reason why elves couldn't have a kingdom or queendom if that was their desire. We've certainly heard from numerous elves throughout our forty plus years journey through these lands in our current incarnation, who are eager to claim to be a king or queen of Elfin. Usually, these are the least suited to that position, but we honor their aspiration and where possible do whatever we can to help them become truly worthy of such titles.

We've even encountered those, although this is rare, who were eager to have a king or queen to rule them. And that is surely their right, although our own feeling was that there was at least of bit of S&M to this desire. Not that we're judging, mind you. To each their own, as we elves say.

In our own experience, the elves we have known who have had communities, even temporary ones, and most are temporary, have sought to create a sort of consensus for decision making. However, the power of personality still had its affect on the situation and there were often various power blocks, this elf allying with that, in order to sway what was going on. But the larger the community gets, the less consensus seems a workable process.

However, what is important and what is vital is that whatever form of government elves choose, it is a matter of choice and that the rights of all individuals, the majority, the minorities (and elven groups tend to be nothing but minorities of various kinds of elves and elfae, anyway), and every individual is protected. Everyone has the right among the elves to choose their form of government, their religion and even their mode of dress and fashion. This does not include, however, the right to force others to be as we think they should be.

Without that, without the choice to be ones'elf and to live in the community of one's choosing, we might as well be men or some other less savory sorts of individuals and would surely, in time, lose our essential elfinness no matter how pointed our ears might be, how beautiful we may appear in the world, or how much we choose to wear traditional elven garb.

~

What do elves think of body modification?

From the elven point of view, body modification, like most things concerning us, is a matter of choice. Our concern is merely that the individual is doing something positive for hir own s'elf, something that heightens hir looks, s'elf esteem, health and improves hir life overall, and this according to hir own understanding and not by our judgments. And, of course, when we speak of body modification we are including piercings, tattoos, scarification and even gender reassignment surgery.

Curiously, in our experience, and we admit that our experience is somewhat limited, elves don't go in for piercings and tattoos as much as pixies seem to do. It is true that we have met and communicated with numerous of our kindred from all over the United States and even some from Europe and other places, but still there are more elves and elfae out there then we know or have encountered and more awakening all the time, so there may very well be elves in the world who are covered in tattoos and pierced up the yin yang.

In fact, we used to know this giant who had been very helpful to these elves who we came across quite by accident one evening when we were just coming out from our local health food store when we lived in Sebastopol, California. He had been gone for a number of weeks on some pilgrimage (he loved to go on pilgrimages) and was very excited about some piercings he had just gotten and wanted to show us since he was so pleased with them. So there in the parking lot that the natural foods store shared with a number of other businesses, including a natural foods restaurant and a video store, just as the evening was coming on and it was getting dark, he whipped out his penis to delightedly display his new piercings. We, of course, being the elves we are, smiled and said, "How nice," while nodding approvingly. Later, we were shaking our heads a bit, not in disapproval so much as the surprising nature of the encounter overall. One never knows what the Universe may reveal.

However, when we say that elves for the most part are less inclined toward tattoos and piercings, it is not to say that there aren't any elves who love tattoos or piercings, or that if you have tattoos or piercings you can't be an elf, only that we as a people tend to do these things less than some of our kin.

Dwarves seem to love tattoos, but they are less interested, for the most part, in piercings. Also, orcs often go in for tattoos, often obtained in prison, but goblins less so and grimlins we've encountered only do so, for the most part, when it is military tattoos, often a skull with, "Kill them all and let God sort them out," emblazoned under it or something similar.

When elves do go in for body modification we tend to go large scale, plastic surgery often, mostly to have our ears made a bit more pointed but also gender reassignment surgery. The number of transgender people we've encountered among our kindred is surely vast compared, it seems, percentage-wise, to the population at large. This is in keeping really with our etheric and spiritual view of race that we have described in earlier sections of this book. Transgender people always have friends among the elves. They are great seers.

This is all to say, dear kindred, that if you have tattoos and piercings and they make you happy then we are happy for you. You don't need our approval to get them, nor anyone else's. This is especially true for elves who do, for the most part, what feels right to us; and society in generally and nearly anyone else can bug off if they don't approve.

"Santa is not only an elf, but a great elf, a Shining One, an immortal spirit, who sets a shining example for all of us to follow."

"We elves not only recognize that Santa is an elf, but also acknowledge him as a great wizard as well."

—— *From the Tomes of Ancient Elven Knowledge*

Chapter 9:
The Language of the Silver Elves: Arvyndase (SilverSpeech)

> We have created our own language, which we call Arvyndase, and have now for decades gifted to our kin over 6,000 elf names in this language. This chapter answers one question we have been asked numerous times, "Do you speak Arvyndase?," along with some other questions about the names we have gifted and the magical use of these names.

Do The Silver Elves speak Arvyndase (SilverSpeech)?

We created an elven language named Arvyndase with a dictionary of over 33,000 entries and a book (*Arvyndase (SilverSpeech): The magical language of The Silver Elves*) that teaches one how to use it in a step-by-step fashion. It took us over ten years to complete the main part of the language, although we still add words from time to time as circumstances dictate. Some folks have asked: do we speak the language? And the truth is we do not. We had thought of learning it but it simply wasn't practical to do so. If we had things we wanted to say in private we could use it as a code but in fact, most of the secrets we have are esoteric in nature and those who don't understand still won't understand even if we told them.

What we do use the language for is spells and in our art pieces, which often have spells in them. We translate our spells into Arvyndase and paint them on our artwork or use them if we have invocations that we are doing. In this way, Arvyndase has been a very useful language to us, lending the sort of mysterious sound and tone to our evocations that Crowley referred to when he spoke of evoking in barbarous languages, although our language we feel is not barbarous but fair and sublime.

Occasionally, one of our kin will write to us in Arvyndase, which is a delight if it isn't too lengthy (looking up a lot of words in our elven dictionary is time consuming and we do prefer to devote a good deal of our time to writing our elven tomes and creating our simple bits of elven art) but it does give us an opportunity to renew our own knowledge of the language and as we elves say, "Never miss an opportunity to learn."

ॐ

How do The Silver Elves create the elf names they gift to others?

Unlike so many others, the elf names we create come to us intuitively. We don't have a formula for creating the names, like those programs that take your world name and transform it or ask you to go by the birthday or month or the first letter of your first and last name and then have a couple of name parts you can put together.

We have been giving magical names for years. Even before we realized we are elves and before we awakened, we were giving our friends magical names. It came to us automatically and naturally, rather than something we decided to do, which is usually a sign that it is a practice and ability that we developed in previous lifetimes. We've been name givers for many, many lifetimes.

Our process, as we said, is primarily intuitive. We read what the individual has written to us about hir (his/her) elfin nature and life and we go over sounds in our minds that feel right to us until we find a name that suits them. Usually, the meaning comes from the person hir own s'elf. What the individual tells us determines the meaning of hir name. But no two elf names are the same either in the name itself or its meaning. Although, of course, they are sometimes similar or related by meaning or sound.

We endeavor to make every name we give a name that will suit the individual to whom we gift one, but we also seek to give them a name that will in some way encourage them and help them. Alas, we know we are not always successful in doing this. Or at least we know that most individuals never use the name we gift them. However, if they do so, it has a power of magic within it that can guide them deeper into Elfin, closer to their own true natures and aid them to discover secrets of Elfin magic that are only revealed in one's dreams.

Of course, some folks like to keep their names secret. They have heard about the power of names and use these names we have given them only in their magic workings and only among those they trust. This we surely understand, but as we explain to people when we give these names, the name we gift is one's true name, it is a sort of code name, one's undercover name, one's elfin secret agent name. It is a sort of passport that admits one entry into the Elfin realms and when one uses it, magic stirs.

∽

Does knowing a person's true name really give you power over hir (him/her)?

This is an old idea but it is more of a metaphor than a direct practical reality. There is no one name that you may have that when known by another person will grant someone power over you, making you into a sort of robot (or into their "bitch" as some so crudely and ignorantly put it). It is true that among the Elf Queen's Daughters we each had a secret name, called the Ba Ka name that only the other sisters of the inner sisterhood knew. But even if others had known the name it wouldn't have granted them any power over us (or made any sense to them, either). The efficacy of this name was in its power to unite us in the sisterhood and make us feel special together. It was an introduction into the inner sisterhood.

If you really wish to speak of a person's true name, then you are actually speaking of the vibration that the individual's body makes, a sort of tone that radiates into the Universe. But even if one could pronounce such a name, while it would allow one to attune to that individual, it still wouldn't give one total power over them (you can't use those Jedi Mind tricks on us).

However, as we said, the true name is a metaphor for understanding the psyche of another individual. If you really understand someone, what sHe (she/he) wants and desires, what motivates hir (him/her), how hir mind works, then yes, you can have great power over that individual and manipulate the individual to do many things, in fact, nearly anything (see I Ching hexagram number 61 or our book *The Elven Book of Changes: A Magical Interpretation of the I Ching*). This is the true meaning of the true name. This is the idea that is expressed in movies and books when someone's children or other loved one is kidnapped and they are told to do this and that or the loved one will die. The individual's true name in this instance is hir love for hir family.

The question we elves ask, however, is why is this power always used for ill? Why is it always, it seems, or mostly used by the wicked? If you know a person's true name, which is to say, if you really understand someone to the point where you can manipulate that individual to whatever you wish, why not use it to further the individual toward the good? To set the individual to do great things? Furthering hir own s'elf and hir others?

This use of the true name is rarely seen in movies and books, although it is not entirely absent. The movie *Cold Comfort Farm*, starring Kate Beckinsale, and the book it is based upon, show an individual doing just this thing, understanding others and setting them toward their true s'elves and fulfillment. In the movie and book, this individual isn't called an elf, and it isn't on the surface a tale about elves, but for the elven it is clearly a magical tale of elfin magic, but then we elves tend to see things that others often don't. We see Elfin and magic where others see but the same old world in the same old way.

What do you do with your elf name?

We have been giving out elf names for those who request them for nearly forty years, each one unique both in the name and its meaning. Yes, all elf names have meaning. Thus far we have gifted over 6,000 names and even have a book filled with over 5,000 of those we've given in order to inspire writers who may need them.

We used to get requests from various novelists and role players asking us to create names for them for their elfae characters. At first, we'd always tell them to be creative and make up their own names, but in time we came to understand that they needed a little tad of help so we put together *The Book of Elf Names* so that they could use the names we created as inspiration for creating their own. That's all they needed really was a touch of guidance.

The fact is, however, although we have created and given out thousands of elf names over the years, very few folks actually use their names. There are several reasons for this, we expect. First, most people don't know what to do with their name and don't understand that by using it they draw magic to thems'elves. Alas, some do try to use it only to find that there are not enough kindred around them that will even accept this new name. This is easier with social media now because one can use an elven name and create an account under that name until someone complains to Facebook and FB forces you to change your name to the one you use for navigating the normal world — the normal names that these elves use to disguise ours'elves. Unfortunately, there is simply not a lot of social reinforcement for using one's elf name and quite a bit of discouragement, so the vast majority abandon them.

Curiously, this is how Zardoa came by his name (although he does have a number of other elf names). It was a name given to a wizard by the Elf Queen's Daughters but that individual never used it. Just threw it into his mystical refuse can, so to speak, where Zardoa found it and said, this is a great name and needs to be used. And was, indeed, perfect for his elfin wizardly identity.

The second reason, however, has to do with the fact that a great many people are just exploring, anyway. They don't really think they are an elf or a faerie, or in fact, they have so little elfin blood in them, or in our point of view elfin spirit, that they are just curious about it all but not really called to Elfin. They've wandered near to the edge of Elfin and they heard its Mystical and Haunting Song and they thought they might just check it out. Rather like someone picking up a guitar or flute and trying to play it for a few minutes but deciding not to pursue it with continuing practice.

And after all, we give the names for free so why shouldn't they check them out? And we, for our part, don't mind. We like creating the names and if an individual doesn't use it then that is up to them. It is a lost opportunity, but then, Elfin is not right for everyone. We simply accept the fact that they were not meant to go deeper into Elfin, or certainly not at this point in their life and evolution and move on to putting energy into and nurturing those who are ready and right for our realms.

For those who do use the names, these names become a power that helps them draw elfin magic to them and enables them to thus step closer toward Elfin. Now it is likely that the name we give them will be just one of many. Elves over time tend to accumulate names. Like most royalty we often have a long list of titles and names that go with them and the longer we tread this path the more we tend to acquire. And often the name we give them is just an introduction. It's like an invitation that one can present at the border of Faerie that says, "Let this one enter."

The real question is: Do you have an elfin Name? And even more importantly: Do you use it? If you would like an elf name gifted to you in the magical language Arvyndase, we invite you to visit our website and follow the directions for doing so at: http://silverelves.angelfire.com/HAelfname.html.

"The Faerie claim that glitter is a language and people who don't understand glitter are 'ilglitterate'."

"We elves name our swords because we believe all things have soul, spirit, power and personality."

"Elves sometimes compare ours'elves to ripe cherries. Shiny on the outside, sweet on the inside, hard in the core. Yet it is that hard seed that gives birth to Evermore."

—— *Elven Words of Wisdom*

Chapter 10:
Oracles of The Silver Elves

> In this chapter we have eight parts, each describing our favorite oracles that we use for magic and personal direction, including: the *I Ching*, tarot, *The Elven Runes*, *Elven Geomancy*, and *The Dream Oracles*, as well as our original divination system *The Elven Star Oracle*.

What oracles do the elves use? Part 1: Tarot

If you ask what oracles the elves use, then we suppose it depends upon the elves you are talking about. Surely we Silver Elves love all sorts of oracles and are always open to using and learning more. We enjoy creating and using some of our own unique divinatory systems like *The Elven Star Oracle* (invoking 88 major constellations) and *The Elven Dream Oracle* (with 360 magical dream symbols). And certainly, and perhaps most often, we read the tarot, which Zardoa first learned when he was about eight years old, although he didn't really get into it deeply until he was in his early twenties. It is one of our favorites, as we expect it is for many elven. Zardoa taught Silver Flame when they first got together and she proved to be a natural.

Although, if you ask what tarot deck we elven like best that again depends upon the individual. We've known elfin who loved decks that didn't move us at all but which they found to be wondrous. For instance, a friend of ours loves the *Xultun Tarot* deck by Peter Balin based upon the Mayan World View. But this deck has, for some reason, never spoken to us at all (although we still own a copy of this deck).

For our own part, we like decks that are beautiful, that have a truly different picture or symbolic representation for each card (which is essentially the primary contribution of the *Waite-Rider* deck to tarot cards) and which tells us something unique or different that we can learn from or which evokes our psyche and challenges us, like dreams do, to understand their meaning. Most decks are actually a variation of the *Waite-Rider* deck, but there are some very good ones out there.

One of the decks we love, even though it isn't strictly a tarot deck, and there are more and more of these types of decks becoming available, is the *Fortune Teller's Mah Jongg* by Derek Walters, which is an interesting oracle. We also love and use periodically John Matthews' the *Celtic Shamans Pack*, Phillip and Stepanie Carr-Gomm's *The Druid Animal Oracle*, Liz and Colin Murray's *The Celtic Tree Oracle*, Jamie Sams and David Carson's *Medicine Cards*, Caroline Smith and John Astrop's *Elemental Tarot*, Nik Douglas and Penny Slinger's *The Secret Dakini Oracle* (one of our favorites), and James Wanless and Ken Knutson's *Voyager Tarot*. And there is a deck we only use when the shit hits the fan and we don't know exactly where we are going next or what to do and that is the *Tele-Psychic Power Cards*, which were printed in Singapore, but whose author is unknown. This deck is a set of affirmation cards that help us keep our heads together in difficult times, although they do tend to be a bit traditional at times, referring to "god," etc. But that is no problem for these elves who simply say Divine Magic instead, making the deck suit our own needs and elven philosophy, as we do all things. And these are just some of our favorites.

We even created our own tarot deck but because it is handmade it is a bit cumbersome to use. Instead, we wrote a book in which you could take any tarot deck or even a regular playing card deck and turn it into an elven oracle. In fact, we entitled it *The Voice of Faerie: Making Any Tarot Deck into an Elven Oracle*. And because we spent a number of years burning candles and drawing cards each day for magic (most of the decks we used for this were given to us by our daughter), we wrote *The Elven Book of Powers: Using the Tarot for Magical Wish Fulfillment* to help those elfin who wished to do the same thing.

At one time we owned over 100 tarot and tarot-like decks, but when we migrated to Hawaii we reduced that number quite a bit. Most of those decks we had purchased used (or we suppose these days we should call them pre-owned) at a local Swap Meet where we sold used (pre-owned) hippie-gypsy-elfin-costume clothes for cheap, along with incense, oils and some imports, and did tarot readings for one dollar a reading (full Celtic Spread) for over 15 years.

Our point is, however, that we love tarot, as do many other elves and are always open to new and interesting decks. And also that the deck that is best for a person, is the one or ones that speak to you. But there are other oracles besides tarot that these elves regularly use and we will get into that next in part 2.

᪇

Beside the tarot what other sort of oracles do elves use? Part 2: I Ching

While the tarot is one of our favorite oracular devices and surely the one we have used for the longest in our lives (over 60 years, yes, we're that old), the oracle that we trust the most, that we use daily and use whenever we encounter any serious difficulty or have an important decision to make, is the *I Ching* (see our book *The Elven Book of Changes: A Magical Interpretation of the I Ching*).

Our sisters of the Elf Queen's Daughters taught us how to do the *I Ching* (as well as teaching us how to do basic astrological charts and giving us the tools for doing so). We had done the *I Ching* previously once or twice before we first met them, but we hadn't really known how to draw the oracle, except in the simplest of ways and didn't have any idea how to draw the individual lines that accompany each hexagram.

The Elf Queen's Daughters (EQD) used the "Ching" regularly, as well. Every single day, every time we in the EQD got together, and every time we visited someone, we'd find a quiet place, first thing, often out in nature somewhere, sit in a circle and do the *Ching* together, each elf drawing a part of the oracle and then passing the sticks to the next person round the circle until the oracle was done.

Alas, while these Silver Elves have tried to teach other elves over the years how to use this oracle, most have been very resistant to doing so. Some complained about the rather sexist and chauvinist attitudes of some of the translations, which were for the most part merely trying to accurately reflect ancient Chinese culture and which is also why we created our own translation that uses non gender pronouns and is geared toward elven culture and magic. Other elves simply said that the system was too complicated for them, although these were usually very intelligent folks and complicated simply wasn't a satisfactory explanation for their resistance. However, we don't strive to force people to do what they don't wish. We, ours'elves, find the *I Ching* to be the most reliable oracle that we know of, but if others don't see the value in using it, that is really their loss. Perhaps they will discover it in a future life.

It is possible that some might feel that being of Chinese origin that it is not elven enough, but there has always been a rather Taoist aspect to the elves, although not Taoism as it has been developed into a religion but Taoism as a philosophy of living in harmony with Nature and of magic. It should be remembered that the *I Ching* comes from a time, thousands of years ago, when the Chinese were not one people, but a variety of tribes, often at odds with each other. Its origins are shamanic and come from so far back in history that there is no real written record of its beginnings, although we do know that it was most likely originally done using tortoise shells and not yarrow sticks, which was a later development. And it is important to note that Chinese culture has its myths and tales of faeries as do most other cultures in the world. The idea that elves and faeries are a strictly Western, even Celtic invention, is simply not accurate.

So, beloveds, if you wish to learn and use a truly great and accurate oracle, we highly recommend the I Ching.

☙

What oracles do elves use? Part 3: Runes

Runes are letters. Every alphabet is a form of runes and could be formulated into an oracle of some sort. There was a time when the ability to read and write were truly seen as magical powers, unlike today when such an ability seems more commonplace. However, when you think about it, you still spend years in school learning to read and write, just as the Druids did, for instance, and it is still a great power. It's just that these days, for the most part, we tend to recognize this power primarily in great literature. When we read a really great book, one that evokes our imagination or sets us thinking about the possibilities of the future, and inspires us in some way, then we really get a sense of the power of Runes used in the form of Grammarye, or the spell of great writing and the magic of good writers.

What is nice about Runes, unlike most other alphabets, is that it is still seen as magical, although Hebrew has also retained its mystical traditions and has many followers and scholars of its systems of Gematria, Temurah and Notariqon. Alas, these elves are not among them, although we have a rudimentary and rather simplistic understanding of these systems.

We did, however, create our own elven rune system. See our *The Book of Elven Runes*, although we might have done better entitling it The Elven Book of Runes, or the Book of Elfin Runes, because we have learned through time that many folks seeing our title leap to the notion that it says the Book of Eleven Runes, but then in German the word for "eleven" is "elf," so there is, perhaps, some deeper connection there.

We have a somewhat similar experience with a tee shirt that Zardoa wears at times that says, "Kiss Me I'm Elvish," on it (he is wearing it on the cover of our book *Elven Geomancy*). However, many folks only observe that it is a green shirt and see the kiss me part and then say things like, "Oh, I'm Irish, too," never bothering to actually read what is said, which is the way a lot of people go through life anyway, ever jumping to conclusions and never looking deeper. But that is, indeed, what oracles are for, a deeper look into the more obscure places in the magical cosmos.

For the most part, these elves don't tend to use our Elven Runes in the same way we use the Tarot or the I Ching, inquiring about day-to-day questions, or deep inquiries prompted by some stressful situation, although we sometimes use them as a supplement to these oracles — an additional point of view, one might say.

Instead, we tend to use the Runes in coordination with some magic we are doing. Often putting them on some sigil or seal we may be creating, or a part of an elven magical circle, or some other bit of artwork that both decorate and magnetize, we might say, our eald/elven home. Sometimes we engrave them on magic wands or staffs that we have created to enhance their magic. And certainly when we have spiritual questions, questions that concern our elven path, we will consult them. There is a magic to them, and we admit we love them, but then, we love nearly all oracles and every form of elven magic. They help remind us of who we truly are in a world that is trying so very hard to make us forget.

What oracles do elves use?
Part 4: Geomancy

One of the things that appeals to us as elves is variety. Thus in our use of oracles, we not only like to use a number of different tarot decks, but also the I Ching, the Elven Runes and also Geomancy, in that way, being able to see a question from a number of different perspectives. Geomancy, which comes from the root words geo, meaning Earth, and -mancy, meaning divination, technically means divination from the Earth, which is an idea that in itself appeals to these Elfin. Alas, the old formulation of Geomancy seemed a bit limited to us, so we created our own version (*Elven Geomancy: An Ancient Oracle of the Elfin Peoples for Divination and Spell Casting*) that gives us a much wider range of possible outcomes. We did the same with our *Book of Elven Runes*.

Traditionally, one made a series of lines consisting of dots in the sand (thus the geo part) and counted if they were odd or even. Since we live in an apartment building, we've found it easier to use dice or stones or coins to arrive at a result. You could, of course, use a pencil or pen and make a series of dots on a piece of paper. Or even use tarot cards or playing cards to achieve a result. And these are all equally effective means of arriving at a result.

But we confess, we are still intrigued by the idea that one might create the oracle naturally. Say if one scooped a palm full of water and then walked and let it drip from one's hand and then counted the dots that had been created. But that is still when one is looking for an oracle. Striving to get an answer. As for instance when one consults the tarot with a question in mind.

With Geomancy, however, it is quite possible that one would simply come across an oracle without asking a question. Just getting a message from Nature and the Spirits. For instance, we used to live in a house in Northern California, before we relocated to the islands in the Uttermost West, and every morning we'd go out and find snail trails crisscrossing the sidewalk. What if we had counted up the dots (or dashes) of the iridescent snail routes and used that in order to receive a geomantic message from the otherworld? That seems to us to be a pretty cool idea.

The same might be done with a number of different things: the number of shells on a particular section of a beach, or the number of holes in a tree from a woodpecker, or various other indicators. This is what really appeals to us about Geomancy. That it is, in its way, so flexible. One just needs to look around one and the signs are everywhere.

∾

What oracles do elves use? Part 5: The Elven Star Oracle

We, like many, perhaps most elves, love oracles and divination. We love doing them. We love experiencing them. And we even love puzzling out their meanings when the answer we have gotten to a question is truly esoteric and mysterious. They stretch our minds and imaginations. Tarot cards and the I Ching are surely our favorites and while we have a passing acquaintance with palmistry, also known as Chiromancy, it has never really intrigued us as much as the Tarot has, although like the use of cards for fortune telling, we began doing palmistry at a very early age. And unlike the tarot or other oracles, it doesn't require one to carry around a deck. Thus we have been at parties or other gatherings and read someone's palm on a moment's notice.

Because of our elven nature, and the fact that much, perhaps most of what applies to our elven culture has been lost through the ages of persecution by more dominant and dominating cultures, we have taken the tarot, runes, *I Ching* and other oracles and made them our own. Giving them our own interpretations with a more elven, and often in some cases, a more magical slant. And in some cases, as for instance the *I Ching*, we've removed the patriarchal bias that is part of their traditional formulation and is just not a part of elven culture. Our culture is based principally upon equality, but if we did have a tendency, it would be more toward a matriarchy rather than a patriarchy. But the strict division of male and female that have been so much a part of the cultures of mankind is not really a part of the elven culture and those who make it seem so are merely drawing us closer to the cultures of mankind and others and away from the true nature of Elfin. We don't deny them their right to do so, if that is their choice, but choice is always the primary aspect of our elven life.

There are, of course, elven tarot decks in the world today in as much as having pictures of elves or faeries or gnomes on a deck makes it elven or elfin. But most of these, like most actual decks overall, are just versions and variations of the *Waite-Rider* deck, and have nothing particularly elven nor even in many cases inspiring about them. Still, they can be fun and in as much as they remind us of Elfin, our elven culture and our elvish kindred, they can be quite helpful and interesting. And while these elves may not find a particular deck interesting, it is quite possible that some other elf will gain greatly from it. We don't presume that our tastes are universally held, even among elves.

And while our elven runes and our version of the *I Ching* are quite useful to us, and a great addition to any divination session, we still hungered for an oracle that was uniquely elven. Something that was completely our own, born of our own magic and culture. Thus we created *The Elven Star Oracle: A System of Divination for Star Enchanters* that utilizes a board that one creates (or could even draw in the sand in times of need) and that one throws stones upon (instructions for making and using the board as well as an illustration of the board and stones are included in the book). *The Elven Star Oracle* is our original divinatory system invoking the 88 major constellations and the blessings of the Shining Ones for guiding one through the world and ever closer to the realization of Faerie. It is called *The Elven Star Oracle* because it is based upon the seven pointed Elven Star, sometimes called the Faery Star, and the areas between the points, overlaid on the dimensional manifestation of Faerie and the realms that are linked to it.

It could surely be used as one's primary oracle, particularly when communicating with or about the Elfin and Faerie realms, although we are still inclined to use the tarot in various forms and the *I Ching* as our primary source of divination and to supplement them with our Runes and Star Oracle, as well as others. Doing so gives us a more complete picture and a more thorough answer and this is particularly true when the answer we first receive is somewhat puzzling.

Rather than simply doing the oracle over again with the same deck or doing the *I Ching* again immediately concerning the same question (something that we've found with the *I Ching* to be particularly ill advised because the answers will just get more and more painful to hear) we use these oracles to give us a fuller picture, while not contradicting the original oracle we received. It is in this way our means of simply asking the oracles to say more and give a fuller picture, a more in depth explanation. Still, in the end, it is always we elfin ours'elves who must interpret the answers given according to our own experience and understanding and there is simply no way to get around this, nor would we wish to do so really.

What oracles do elves use? Part 6: Miscellaneous

As we've said elsewhere, these elves love all sorts of oracles, and we think among those who enjoy doing or having oracles done, that this is probably true for most folks. Certainly, there will be those who prefer this oracle to that. Those who have their preferred means of doing or receiving oracles, but we expect, without having done a scientific study to see if this is so, that most of us are intrigued by a variety of forms of divinations. These elves, for our own part, are very fond the Tarot and the *I Ching*, but love to learn and see other techniques done. We've even known elves to use

Bibliomancy, which is opening a book at random and letting one's finger fall on a sentence or word. We've surely done this ours'elves just for the fun of it.

But there are also books that can be used for oracles that are not necessarily oracle books. One of these, for instance, is our *An Elfin Book of Spirits*, which is designed for conjurors so we might call spirits to aid (and abet) us. One might, if one so chooses, go through the book and find the spirit that is right for the magical task one has in mind. However, these elves like to use a divination system, which we explain in that book, and toss stones to see which spirit we get at random. Then if we get a spirit that especially suits our quest, we take it as a very good sign. Although, sometimes we get a spirit whose expertise seems totally different than the task we have in mind. We still assume this is the right spirit for the job, but we are then called to reflect upon why that particular spirit would be so. It challenges our imaginations the same way a dream or a surprising response from the Tarot might do so and we love puzzling out dreams.

Another of this sort of oracle is our *The Elven Book of Dreams*, which is designed to help elves understand thems'elves and others by associating the degree of the Sun sign, the Moon, Jupiter or any other planetary body or aspect of one's horoscope and getting a response about it that illuminates the individual's nature and hir evolutionary path. But this can also be used, utilizing the same set of stones that we use for randomly drawing spirits, to obtain an oracle. This book, simultaneously, has spell chants that can be used to help one achieve one's goals.

And similar, in certain ways, is our book *The Shining Ones*, that is designed to help one find the Shining One, the angelic elven spirit that guides one, much in a way of a guardian angel, and overlooks one's life course and development, according to one's birthday. One could, in fact, pick any date or day of the year, say the date one is getting married or starting a business or job, etc., and find what Shining One rules that date and in that way also obtain a sort of oracle for one's quest.

We could say using these books in this way is a sort of Bibliomancy. Only instead of opening the book at random (although you could still do so) one uses stones or in the case of the Shining Ones, picks a date that is relevant to one's quest or spiritual evolution. As Aleister Crowley pointed out in his book *Magick Without Tears*, the whole Universe is like a book that we can read, seeing the omens and oracles and hidden meanings that exist all around us. We just need to learn the methods for reading this most wondrous and esoteric of languages, the Language of the Universe, the Chant of the Stars, and the Song of Elfin.

What oracles do elves use? Part 7: Magic the Gathering

We used to sell hippie, gypsy, costume, elfin faerie clothes, along with incense, candles and various other trinkets at a local swap market each weekend and Zardoa would do tarot readings for a dollar, that is for a basic Celtic spread reading and a dollar for each question after that. We were rather famous in the area and had numerous regular costumers as well as people who would be floating through and just give it a try for the hell of it.

One day a couple came and got a reading and afterward they wanted their young son to have a reading as well, but he wasn't interested. Seeing from what the boy was holding in his hands that he had just come back from a booth where they sold *Magic the Gathering* cards, Zardoa said, "I'll read those for you," indicating that he would use the *Magic the Gathering* cards to do the reading. This peaked the boy's interest and he immediately handed over the deck he had just created from the cards he'd just purchased. Zardoa shuffled them and, as is the manner of elven readings, he let cards jump out and read them for the lad, using the basic Celtic spread for the reading.

As an aside, we have tried various other spreads over the course of the years but found that since most people are familiar with the Celtic spread that this was also what they were most comfortable with so that is what we nearly always used for the general public when reading.

It turned out to be a pretty good reading that both the boy and the parents enjoyed and the *Magic the Gathering* deck, while it was composed in this case of a number of cards that were identical, none-the-less proved to be a pretty interesting deck for reading.

And this is our point, nearly any deck can be used as an oracle. You can certainly use a regular playing deck. There are even books on that subject. And this is how Zardoa began doing readings when he was very young. Well, first his mother got him a *Gypsy Witch Fortune Telling Deck* when he was about eight years old and attending military school, but he found after that that he might be at some party or gathering and there was nearly always a playing deck available that he could use for readings and if not that then he could always read their palms.

Zardoa could even use baseball cards. Do they still exist? That is to say if he knew anything about baseball, which he doesn't. Or really, he could use any other deck where he has some knowledge concerning the cards or the graphics are at least inspiring.

When he was young and all the other boys were collecting baseball cards he collected History cards, which were cards that had a picture on one side and the other explain some historical person or event the picture illustrated. Surely, those cards don't exist anymore but if they did they'd make for some very interesting readings.

~

What oracles do elves use? Part 8: Necromancy

Mancy is a word that refers to divination and Necro- deals with the dead, so Necromancy is talking to or really communicating with the dead. One of the most famous examples of Necromancy comes from the Old Testament when King Saul goes to the Witch of Endor and has her summon up the dead prophet Samuel. Television and Movies often extend Necromancy to mean magic done by evoking the dead but we elves would call that Necromagery rather than Necromancy (see our book *Ruminations on Necromancy: Continuing Correspondence Between the Silver Elves and the Founders of the Elf Queen's Daughters* for more on this).

As far as Necromancy goes, every time you speak to a deceased parent or grandparent you are engaged in Necromancy, particularly if you get a response from them in return. The Honoring of our Ancestors, which can be found in nearly every culture in the world, is also essentially a form of Necromancy.

Of course there are mediums who speak with the dead and others that channel living entities from other dimensions, but really the most common and popular method of Necromancy is surely the Ouija board. Zardoa used a Ouija board for a time when he was in undergraduate school and was rather good at it really, but it never quite gave him the satisfaction that using the Tarot did and he soon abandoned it.

The Elf Queen's Daughters, on the other hand, were really quite adept at the use of the Ouija board and sometimes when we would visit the Fox River Vortex Melryn and Andruil would sometimes retreat together into the attic and use the board to communicate with their contact on the spirit planes. They obtained a temporary Bah Kah name for Zardoa that way. Every member of the inner sisterhood of the Elf Queen's Daughters had a secret Bah Kah name that was known only to the other sisters. Later, Arwen and Elanor, who founded the sisterhood would give him his permanent Bah Kah name and also one for Silver Flame, again using Necromancy via the Ouija board to do so.

In fact, as we've mentioned in some of our books, it was via that Ouija board that they first received the message to found the Elf Queen's Daughters in Carbondale, Illinois in 1973-4. They had known a woman that they were quite close to, who had died while saving children from a burning house, whom they used as their contact. They sometimes told a story about when she was alive. Some months before her death, they had been traveling together when they came upon a group of Romany/Gypsies who when seeing this woman began giving her pieces of paper with messages for the spirits on the other side. This experience puzzled them at the time but somehow the Romany knew she was about to pass over.

Arwen and Elanor were kind enough to let us view some of their Necromancy sessions, something that usually took place in private. And Silver Flame particularly proved quite adept at using the Ouija board. However, in the long run of things we found that we still liked the Tarot a great deal better, as well as the daily use of the *I Ching* (something they also taught us how to do and which they also did regularly) and we let our Ouija exercises fall to the wayside. It just wasn't quite for us.

On the other hand, we still speak to the departed spirits, mostly guiding them toward new lives and then blessing them and nurturing them on the astral and spiritual planes as they begin those lives so they can overcome some of the obstructive foibles, prejudices and bad habits of their previous lives, avoid some of the negative experiences that caused those habits to develop in the first place and at the same time sending them blessings so they will be far more successful in a positive way at those things they aspired and which we expect, knowing them, that they continue to desire to achieve. And occasionally, we might get some sign from them, some indication that they hear us and appreciate our help. But mostly our messages come from the Shining Ones who guide us and thus guide the dead/reincarnating souls through us.

Chapter 11: Other Miscellaneous Questions About Being an Elf

> Most of the questions in this book about being an elf and following the elven way were asked to us through the years either in person or through email, and later in private Facebook messages by our elven sisters and brothers. As you will see, the questions in this chapter cover a variety of topics from concerns about elves and iron, gardens and wild spaces, relationship to *Dungeons and Dragons*, and even being in prison.

Does iron burn elves?

It is a tradition in some fairy lore that iron burns elves and faerie folk. We suspect that this is a reflection of the fact that since our folk were earlier peoples and probably used stone tools, or perhaps copper or silver tools, that iron, which is a harder metal, was a bit of an anathema to us at first. However, we've also considered that since many early invaders, such as the Saxons, had a great deal of lore about elf bolts and elf arrows and how they are poisoned both magically and possibly by herbs, that this is just a switching of the roles so that while they are poisoned by our magic, we are to their minds poisoned by their iron.

However, we've never known any elves who were actually allergic to iron, although we surely don't discount the possibility that some elven sisters and brothers may be allergic to iron (particularly in jewelry) and we do know of some who can not take iron as a supplement internally because they already have enough or too much of this essential mineral in their bodies. What we have also encountered from time-to-time, are elves and fae who claim they are allergic, even when they are not, because that is what the lore says of us and thus they wish to harmonize with the lore in order to prove that they are elven. In fact, we once went out to an elegant dinner with a young elf lass who forgot her silverware that she usually carried with her and refused to use the stainless steel cutlery that the restaurant offered and insisted on eating with her fingers because of this very desire to prove her elven nature.

It is possible that, in time, if she kept up this habit that she would, indeed, develop a psychosomatic reaction to iron but that would only be the case if she actually knew that she was handling iron. There is a mental disorder called Somatoform that causes symptoms and pain in an individual who believes they have a particular disease even though tests find there is no evidence, other than the symptoms, of them having the disease. It is an extreme form of hypochondria. In the course of generations this disorder, if carried on by a family, could produce a mutation in which a group of elves would be allergic to iron.

But our question is: why would we want such a thing? Why would we embrace and cling to a weakness instead of seeking to overcome it? And again, the answer is that some folks, who psychologically and sometimes hidden to their own s'elves, doubt their elven nature, which is easy thing to happen in this world where we are surrounded by individuals who deny our identity, thus cling to the various aspects of the ancient lore to prove they are elven. To their minds if they are allergic to iron then that's the proof that they must be elven. But truly, beloved kin, we have no obligation to prove ours'elves to anyone. If others do not see or accept our elven or fae nature that is truly their loss for the wonder and the blessing that would have been theirs is ignored. This is like coming across a huge diamond and thinking it is a worthless piece of glass.

This reminds us a bit of the vampires that the main character in Anne Rice's *Interview with a Vampire* encountered when he went to Paris and found that the vampires there were afraid and allergic to crosses because they believed they could be harmed by these items. The truth was, however, that it was only their belief that gave the cross or holy water any power over them. So why would elves wish to be vulnerable to iron? If Superman could overcome his vulnerability to Kryptonite, wouldn't he do so? If we elves, for the most part, ever were allergic to iron, it is no longer so. At least, not for the majority of us, who have evolved beyond such weakness and thus made ours'elves stronger and less vulnerable. Embrace your strengths, beloved, and seek to overcome your weaknesses, thus will we survive, evolve and grow into the Light of Elfin where our future awaits us.

For more on the Elven associations for Iron, see our *The Book of Elven Runes* and in particular Rune # 7, Iron.

"Nature adorns us." — *Olde Elven Saying.*

Do elves have green thumbs?

We used to joke that we had black thumbs, since nearly everything we tried to grow dropped dead. This is not entirely true, actually. We found in the course of time that plants that required little attention from us, such as succulents, and plants that were fairly hardy, such as spider plants, did pretty well with us. Otherwise, we just couldn't figure out how much water they needed, often overwatering them or under-watering them or whatever.

These elves love plants. We just don't have green thumbs. And we used to feel slightly guilty about this because we thought that elves should have green thumbs and a tremendous ability to grow plants, but in our case this just wasn't so. (Actually, we've come to believe it is mostly the faeries that have green thumbs). We are not particularly great gardeners, but we do like to grow plants now and then when we can. We have about a half dozen growing in our apartment at this moment. Two of them are trees. Not tall as yet, but growing.

It is true that plants that live with us are better off if they can mostly take care of thems'elves and one of the things we've learned in tending to them is to leave them alone for the most part. They are, overall, a rather quiet folk. We do greet them each day and they silently acknowledge us, but mostly they like to bask in the sun, the extroverts, or hide in the shade, the introverts, and be left to their own devices, which is okay with us. An occasional bit of watering is all they really desire from us and they kindly give us oxygen in return as well as just the delight of being able to see them develop.

Then we read Nicholas De Vere's *The Dragon Legacy*, which

said that elves didn't have green thumbs since they were breed to be leaders not farmers and that instead it was their client peoples, those that hired them to govern, that had green thumbs. And we thought, okay, that works for us. Although, we expect that the truth is that De Vere, like us, just wasn't much good with plants and was projecting his own lack of ability upon all elven folk.

There is a tendency for people, including elves when they are beginning to awaken, to assume all other elves are like them, but since elves are unique beings, individually and collectively, this is seldom true. What seems more likely to us is that some elves have green thumbs and others not and this has very little to do with our elvenness, other than we do, for the most part, love nature and we expect that quite a few of us that don't have green thumbs wish that we did. And we expect that if we keep attempting to grow plants (poor plants) we will, like all relationships where people care and wish to make it work, improve our skills in doing so.

Even if we look at Tolkien's creation of the Valar and Maiar, we'd see that these are beings with different skills and personalities, some of whom might be very good with plants and others less likely to be so. We all have our skills and, as elves, we all seek to develop our skills whatever they may be. So, beloved, if you are one of those who isn't very good with plants as yet, don't worry. If you truly wish to be, you will develop that skill in time; and if it doesn't really interest you, you are no less an elf for having other interests. We won't say that we can't all be great gardeners. If we put our minds to it, we surely could be. But the simple fact is that we don't all care to be so and that is perfectly okay.

And for those elves who do have green thumbs, we much admire you and despite what De Vere writes, you are no less elven for having that wondrous ability to commune with the flora.

☙

Do elves prefer gardens or wild places?

Like most things that have to do with elves, the answer is both. Elves love the wild places and elves love beautiful gardens. However, the answer as nearly always is also: it depends upon the individual elf. Some elves may love wild places and not care for gardens and others may be garden lovers but are shy or uninterested in venturing into the wild. There is no one that says that we need to be one way or the other and if there is then they really don't understand elves.

For our own part while we Silver Elves like gardens, particularly botanical gardens, even though we seem to be absolutely incapable of creating them. Even on a very small scale, it just doesn't seem to work for us and honestly, we're just not that motivated to do it, which may be in part why this is so.

Instead, these elves just tend to let things run wild. If we weren't compelled by society to cut our lawns (in those circumstances when we do have lawns) we just wouldn't do so. We used to live a bit out in the country in Northern California and our yard would often have three to four foot high weeds growing all over it. We did have neighbors, however, and they requested we do a little mowing so we got a large scythe, like you often see Death holding, or in the pictures of Father Time at the new year, and Zardoa would go out occasionally and use it to mow the weeds down to a more acceptable height of about six to 10 inches.

Our English neighbors, who referred to us as The Magics, found it particularly hilarious to watch Zardoa out scything our large back yard. And we must say, they, for their part, had an incredible garden of flowers and edible plants. It was wondrous for sure. A beauty to look at but simply beyond our abilities to create.

As we explained in the last section, if plants can't take care of thems'elves for the most part, they are unlikely to survive among these elves. So we don't do flower gardens, unless you consider wildflowers popping up here and there as a flower garden and we don't do vegetable gardens unless they are what we call volunteer gardens.

Even though we don't garden in any intentional or formal way, we do create compost heaps in which we toss all our organic waste and often we have found that plants, especially squash of many varieties, just voluntarily pop up and grow there and if they do we will water them occasionally as they seem to need it and we have had many a fine squash dinner thanks to the kindness of the squash faeries. And occasionally other things have grown as well. We once grew our own pineapple.

And in the residence previously mentioned where we were scything the yard, we came upon some grape vines that the landlord had uprooted and left to die from another part of the property and although it had been about a week before we got to them, we planted them by our back porch and in due time had wonderful organic grapes growing over a large trellis that we created.

But the point here is if you are a garden elf (like a garden gnome?) or a wild elf (with pixie blood like us), you are equally beloved and should feel very good about yours'elf for you are surely perfect as you truly are and need not feel guilty if you can't make a garden work nor feel inadequate if you are not that enamored by venturing into the wild. Be true to your own s'elf, dear kin, and you will be embraced by Elfin and your kindred elves.

☙

Do Silver Elves only exist in Dungeons and Dragons books?

We recently posted a notice of one of our books that had just been published on a group site on Facebook and this guy responded to us in a rather hostile fashion, accusing us of this and that and the other thing, which we will get to more thoroughly in a future chapter, as well as impugning our motives for writing our books in the first place, but first of all by stating that Silver Elves only exist in *Dungeons and Dragons* books.

However, when we asked this individual whether he had ever actually read any of our books he replied, "I don't read fictions (sic)." (We knew right then that he had never even read 'about' our books since most of our books are non-fiction.) And then when we pointed out that he might be more knowledgeable about what we really wrote if he'd actually read some of our books, he said, "I didn't say I hadn't," which seemed to contradict his earlier statement. Unfortunately, before we could reply to that inconsistency, he deleted his whole response and this was just at the point where we were beginning to have a bit of fun with him.

Here though, we wish to deal with his very first objection to us, which is the fact that we call ours'elves The Silver Elves and use that as a nom-de-plume as well as s'elf identification. We have called ours'elves other things over the last 40+ years we've been on this Elven Path including the Elves of the Southern Woodlands when we were a vortex of the Elf Queen's Daughters living in Southern Illinois and the Sylvan Elves when we lived in Northern Florida.

Now, it is possible that he meant that Silver Elves only exist in *Dungeons and Dragons* but other types of elves actually do exist in the world, although we doubt that is what he intended. We assume that his objection was to us referring to ours'elves as elves at all. After all, he didn't believe in elves and therefore to his mind we didn't have a right to believe in ours'elves either. Like so many people in the world, he wished to tell us what we are or aren't and expected us to conform to his definition of us. But then while we've listened to other folks' opinions of us, we've never really heeded them to the point of letting them define us, and if we did then we really wouldn't be elves, would we?

It has always been our assertion that if anyone has a right to define what elves are, it should be we who are elven, not those who are not and certainly not those who claim we don't exist, often to our very faces. Of course, they would say we are only claiming to be elves, but really we are not just claiming we are elves, we are being elves, day by day and often more importantly, night by night. This is to say, we live our lives as elves, which means that we are elves by magic, that is to say by action and manifestation, if in no other way. And how else would a person expect elves to come into being, if not by magic?

On the other hand, we don't insist that others believe we are elves anymore than we would insist that someone be our friend. That is simply not possible. Nor do we insist that our friends even believe that we are elves, they just have to be friendly. But surely part of being friendly is recognizing that we call ours'elves elves because we love everything that is elfin and fae and to our minds that in itself tends to indicate we are elves. Who else but elves would be so fanatically obsessed with elves? So we don't expect our friends to believe us but we do expect them to at least humor us a bit. After all, we accept that they believe all the crazy stuff that they do, and smile and love them dearly.

What would you say to an elf in prison?

As far as being a prison elf that hardly defines you. We are all prisoners of this world, trapped in matter, and even more trapped in the enculturated belief and habit patterns that the world offers us. Most folks in prison, we expect, as in the outer world, are merely fulfilling role models that have been set before them from ages long past. In many ways, except for having to interact with very unenlightened individuals on a daily basis, your life isn't entirely unlike that of monks (who also, sometimes, have to deal with the unenlightened at times as well as strict and limiting rules of living). Although, we ours'elves have never been in prison, except to participate as guests in The Game at Marion Federal Penitentiary many ages go, so our understanding of what you encounter and the pressures you are under is extremely limited.

Of course, unlike most who might be of the Buddhist/monkish variety of elves, which is to say, those who feel we should do all we can to evolve beyond the material world, these elves are of the notion that we need to learn to master the world, not through force but through enchantment, and not by working outwardly so much as developing our powers inwardly. Having said that, like all else in life, saying is much easier than doing, also a great deal quicker. We, like you, struggle each day to improve ours'elves and to become better as elven spirits and soulful beings and as far as we can see we are many lifetimes away from achieving even our most humble goals. This is where perseverance becomes essential and endurance a most subtle and great power.

˜

Do Elves really follow their Dreams?

Usually when one speaks of following their dreams, one is speaking of the idea that one has an ambition, often of a creative nature, that one pursues in the world despite all obstacles. And surely this is true of elves that we have pursued our dream of Elfin in spite of all those who have ridiculed us and those who simply don't believe in Elfin or that we are elves or even have the courtesy to acknowledge that being elven is our chosen identity whether they believe in elves or not.

And when we say "in spite of" there is surely some truth to that in a literal sense. The opposition of the normal folk has made us even more determined than ever to follow our dreams. However, even with such opposition, we would still endeavor, each and every day, to live our lives as the elves we are and know ours'elves to be. Our path is essentially positive and not primarily based upon a reaction to others. Yet, we would be

remiss if we didn't admit that their opposition instills us with an even greater sense of purpose.

But when we elves speak of following our dreams, we don't mean it merely as it is popularly considered, as putting energy into our ambitions. We are indicating quite literally that we heed the dreams we have at night, analyze them when they puzzle us or specifically call to us and follow the clues that they give us as best that we are able to do so.

We have already written in another section of this book about the fact that we have interpreted dreams professionally, although there was not nearly the demand for this that there was for our tarot readings, and that we studied for over a year with Jeremy Taylor, the author of *Dream Work: Techniques for Discovering the Creative Power in Dreams* and other works on dreams and dream interpretation.

Most of our dream interpretation, however, concerns our own dreams and what they say to us and we pay close attention to their messages, as we expect most elvish folk do. We even created a dream oracle book, not a dream symbol book, but an oracle that was based upon 360 of Zardoa's dreams. We take our dreams seriously.

From our point of view, our dreams connect us to our ancestors through what Jung would call the Collective Unconscious and the aboriginal elvish of Oz referred to as the Dreaming or the Dreamtime, an archetypal realm where the Shining Ones, as we elves would call them, brought the world into being by virtue of magic, and which exists, like Faerie, in the etheric and astral realms, or as Jung would call it the "Psychoid," along with and within the manifest world that we exist within. The Shining Ones created a series of sacred/magical sites, realms of Elfin and Faeries we might say, that are connected upon the earth by a series of Songlines, that some might call ley lines, but we elves, of course, much prefer the term Songlines that our cousins of Oz use.

Thus for the elves, following our dreams means a great deal more than achieving our personal goals in the world. It means being and remaining in touch with the Divine Magic, the Shining Ones, who are our ancestors and with the our own inner directives and destiny as individual beings and as a people.

And when we pass from this life, we shall return to the Dreaming, to Elfin, from which we have come and where our kindred, who are thems'elves awaiting the right moment to reincarnate, will greet us and we shall share our dreams of an Elfin yet to come and then return again to manifest it through our lives upon the Earth and in the far reaches of Space.

"Stepping into Faerie is like waking from a dream and realizing you're still dreaming."

It is true that Seelie Elves cannot lie?

Actually, this is not true. It makes for an interesting character aspect for Seelie Elves in books and fiction in general but in reality we not only can lie, we are great liars. Some of the best in the world. On the other hand, we much prefer the truth whenever possible and, in fact, almost never lie and only do so when necessary to protect ours'elves and our kindred. Lying is simply a waste of our time and energy. And the truth is so much more powerful anyway. Naturally, we chose the way of power, as nearly any magical people would.

In the stories, they say that while we can't lie that we are eager to deceive people using loopholes and tricky language, rather like some politicians, used car salespeople and real estate agents. This is also not true, although, it is not quite as untrue as the idea that we can't lie at all. Again, we don't strive to deceive people usually. Although, once again, we are willing to do so if they endanger us in some way. However, we prefer not to do so and, in fact, have found deceiving people is totally unnecessary. People for the most part, particularly the normal folk, are so very eager to deceive their selves. They don't want to know the truth, especially about elves and faerie folk and Elfin and Faerie. The truth about us challenges their preconceptions and often their chosen ideologies. In fact, if you tell them the truth, they will openly deny it. They are so habituated to lie and deceive others that they lie to themselves constantly and can't tell truth from fable or myth. To them, every fact that they don't agree with is fake news. It is bad enough that they don't believe we exist, even when we stand before them, but they deny Global Climate Change, plus that women are equal human beings, often superior to men, that animals have minds and souls of their own, that trees are sentient creatures.

With people such as these, telling the truth is almost a waste of breath, although we tell the truth anyway most of the time for as we say it is unnecessary to attempt to deceive them. No matter what we tell them, they will take it and distort it and turn it into something completely different based totally upon their own prejudices, biases and distorted worldviews, putting their own twisted spin on things. Who needs to lie or deceive when others will do the work for you?

In fact, for the most part, we love to tell these folks the truth and watch their faces as they attempt to digest it and frequently get this look on their faces of mental indigestion. It looks a bit like confusion only somewhat more painful. They must suffer from near continual mental heartburn. Talk about cognitive dissonance! And that's the truth, beloved, we would not lie to you.

༄

Do the elves love poetry?

There is a good deal of poetry in Tolkien's works and one gets the idea that poetry was very important to the ancient folk, both elven and other sorts of folk. In our own experience, elves often like to write poetry, but we are not always that fond of reading it. We much prefer fiction. But poetry can be fun, as well as a challenge, to write.

These days poetry seems to fall into three categories. A sort of highbrow poetry that one might find in the *Atlantic Monthly*, a sort of hippie poetry that one finds coming from the fringe of society, and the most popular sort of poetry, dirty limericks. These days poetry is not really popular at all, except as it is delivered as music lyrics and then it is very popular, and we elves expect that, in fact, this was always the case.

Poetry is incredibly popular today as it is expressed as rap or hip-hop and in other musical forms. The idea that we elves would sit around reading poetry to each other at a salon, while possible, is less likely than that we will dance to poetry as it sings out of our sound system, or in modern times, the speakers blaring out of a passing car. In that sense, we elves, and nearly everyone else, love poetry, although the nature, style and genre of the poetry differs widely.

Many people argue about their poetry, declaring that the poetry of their generation was better than that of the current generation, but they've been saying that for thousands of years. And others love one sort of poetry and hate others. While we elven often have our preferences for musical poetry, we will listen to it all if it is playing and dance to it if at all possible. And this includes when it is playing in clothing stores, grocery stores and even sometimes on elevators if there is enough room.

This is not to say that we haven't ever sat in an evening soiree and read and listened to poetry. We have on a number of occasions (but we'd have a few drinks by then). Although, while others were reading poetry taken from books selected off a shelf, we were reading poetry we had just written in the course of the evening, inspired by the people and events around us.

In ancient times, our bards would sing poetry to us around the fires, but there weren't books of fiction or not many in those days and there certainly wasn't television or movies. But there was theatre and we elves love theatre and most of all we love good storytellers. But we've, much to the surprise of many folk, have embraced television (the third greatest educational tool ever invented, just behind video games and romance, and we say romance because it motivates us to learn languages and almost every other thing in order to fulfill our romantic dreams) and particularly movies, especially if they are about elves, faeries, magic or hold the mysteries within them. But then it should be said that we see magic where others do not and see Faerie nearly everywhere.

※

What is the Difference between Elven and Elvish?

Some have asked us what the difference is between the words Elven and Elvish and while different elfae may have their own definitions these elves use them to indicate the Elven, which is to say those of us who are elven and identify as being elves and the Elvish, which are all manner of elfin folk, such as the pixies, the brownies, the leprechauns and every sort of elven type and variations thereof, of which there are surely more than we've even encountered as yet for

Elfin is ever expanding and the elves ours'elves and the elvish are ever mutating and creating new and intriguing forms and variations on our culture.

We often use elvish to indicate those who may not even identify as elves or any sort of otherkin but who remind us of our own kind, however way they may see their own selves. Thus we see elvish sorts among the Goth, the Emo, the Vampires, the Streampunkers, Gypsies, Freaks (Hippies) and many other folks. We see elvish kin among the Vulcans and Romulans of Star Trek and in many other places, forms and peoples. Of course, the Romulans tend toward the dark side of Elfin, but we are kin to all our folk and embrace and nurture all that will allow us to do so.

We also use the world Elfae that we created years ago to indicate all of otherkin sorts. The Faeries, the Fay, the Fee, the Fae, the Fey, the Kobolds, TommyKnockers, the Gnomes, Dwarves and every other variation of other that there might be. Some fall on the Seelie or Light side and others on the Unseelie, which some might say Dark side, although really in our experience the difference is between those that tend toward the healing, sharing, loving and nurturing of all humanity and those who tend to be parasitic toward those who are different than they. The Seelie generally strive to understand and enlighten Mankind and others while the Unseelie think those folks deserve whatever they get — or really, whatever they can do to or take from them (of course this is a generalization and not true of all our kin, Seelie or Unseelie).

The word elfin we use in two ways. When we capitalize it as in Elfin, we usually are indicating the place or space that is the elvish part, realms and dimensions of Faerie. Faerie is a vaster realm than Elfin, but Elfin tends to be, usually, a bit more civilized. Certainly, it is safer for the Elfae. If we compared them to our dreams and our Unconscious, Faerie is the vast Unconscious where anything can happen, including nightmares at times. Whereas Elfin tends toward kinder dreams, although usually dreams of magical import, of signs and omens concerning one's path — dreams that connect us and show the way, and dreams that uplift us and give us messages from the Shining Ones.

If you step from Elfin into vaster Faerie, you are surely setting out on an adventure and definitely taking your chances. Although, one can always retreat to Elfin, as one can awaken from a nightmare, and one can ever go forth again when one feels prepared and ready to do so. For most Elfae, stepping into a normal world is equivalent to encountering one's nightmares in a lucid dream and when one is ready that is surely a good thing to do, for we are here to master that world, which is to say to obtain mastery over our own reactions to that world and by doing so shape our lives and our futures.

But when we use elfin, without the capitalization, then we are using it much in the same way we use elvish. We've had people from time to time write to us declaring with great authority that it is elvish not elfin and others that it is elfin not elvish, but such limited points of view are seldom elfin or elvish. We included everything we can into our realms, transforming it as we please and thus we extend the boundaries of Elfin day by day and surely night by night. And you are always welcome to join us.

"Elves say that truth is both absolute and relative. It is absolutely relative and relatively absolute."

— *Elven Koan*

More Old Elven Sayings:

"Elves almost never lie. When circumstances force us to deceive we much prefer to do it with the truth."

"When men were just a twinkle in their mother's eyes, elves were a glimmer on the horizon, a dancing light in the forest, and the shimmer of starlight in the depths of the night."

"Elves are the Voice in the Wilderness."

"At dramatic moments in movies, men often say, 'Come with me if you want to live.' We elves say, 'Come with us if you want to live it up.'"

"The Faeries say that International Faerie day is June 24th, the elves say International Elf day is everyday."

Chapter 12:
The Silver Elves Books

As you may know by now, we have over 40 books on magic and enchantment and the Elven Way. Most of these books are non-fiction, but we do also have one novel, a book of short story otherkin fairy tales, and two books of elven poems. People are always asking us which of our books is best to read for this and that various interests, be it about elven magic, elven philosophy, elven lifestyle, elven oracles, elven personal myth, or elven language. So this chapter (which we submit to you really as an appendix to this book) is dedicated to answering these questions about which of our books to read, and also some miscellaneous questions about our books that people have asked us from time-to-time.

What book by The Silver Elves should I start with?

We actually get asked this question quite a bit and we usually answer by asking what the individual is interested in, since our books cover a variety of topics (although all elven and faerie) and are meant in a way and as much as we are able to explore various aspects of elven culture as widely as we may. In a certain sense we are laying the foundation for the re-awakening Elven Culture.

At the same time, if you are reading this and this is your first book of ours to read, then this is surely a very good book to begin with since it references a number of our books and gives a good overview of our writing concerning a myriad of topics of interest to the elven and the awakening and inquiring elfae. From this book you can get a sense of the direction you would like to proceed in pursuing the elven path and increasing your understanding of elven culture, magic and society.

If your interest is in ritual or ceremonial magick, then our *The Book of Elven Magick 1 & 2* are perfect for this, especially when combined with *An Elfin Book of Spirits*. Of course, all our books are magic books in a sense and most of them have little spells of various sorts in them. But for doing Western Ceremonial Magick in an elven way, adapting it to elven forms of magick, then those just mentioned are the best.

If you are looking for elven oracles to help guide your life, we have a number of these, although our own favorite is *The Elven Book of Changes* our elven interpretation of the I Ching. But we also have *The Book of Elven Runes*, *The Elven Book of Dreams*, *Elven Geomancy* and *The Elven Star Oracle*. The first four books are our interpretation of traditional divination systems but the *Star Oracle* is a completely elven and original system and we hope to create more in the future.

For elven cosmology and cosmongony, you may try *Faerie Unfolding* and *Through the Mists of Faerie* and for more on the elven path then you surely would be best served by reading *The Elven Way* and *Liber Aelph*. These are books of elven philosophy but for more practical day-to-day guidance on interacting with other elves and elfae and normals we recommend *What an Elf Would Do*, our book of etiquette; and if you are interested in elven politics and government then we suggest that you read *The United States of Elfin*.

If fiction is your thing, and honestly most elven, but not all, approach our culture mainly through fiction, myth and lore, then our novel *The Elves of Lyndarys*, a book about modern elves, may appeal to you or our short story collection *Elven Silver*. And if poetry is the thing that tickles your fancy, you may wish to check out *Caressed by An Elfin Breeze* and *An Elven Game of Rhymes*. On the other hand, if you are looking for true stories of our lives and magic then we recommend *Eldafaryn* and *Living the Personal Myth*. And if you are looking to discover what sort of elfae you are and the sort of magic you tend toward then *The Elven Tree of Life Eternal* may be quite helpful in this regard.

If you wish to delve into the origins of our particular elven tradition and the Elf Queen's Daughters then you would surely wish to read *The Elf Magic Mail, vols. 1 & 2*, which are the original letters of the Elf Queen's Daughters, and also read our own *Magical Elven Love Letters, vols. 1, 2 & 3* that are a continuation of that series. Also, our letters of correspondence between the founders of the Elf Queen's Daughters and the Silver Elves may also be of interest. These are *Magic Talks, Sorcerers' Dialogues, Discourses on High Sorcery* and *Ruminations on Necromancy*.

Also, in our book *Living the Personal Myth: Making the Magic of Faerie Real in One's Own Life*, more may be read on Elven heritage in general, including our own descent from the Pict-Sidhe (pixies), the Merovingian Fisher Kings (the fae or fairy folk), and the Albigens, the Elven Bloodline. While we do not feel that bloodline is near as important as the spiritual component of being Elven in ones present life, we find the study of the Elven bloodline interesting. We also cover in this book the future prophesy and new mythos of elves with *The Return of Faerie* and *The Starlight Path*.

All of these books and many more may be discovered on our website at silverelves.angelfire.com.

~

What book of yours is best if I'm interested in ... ? Part 1: Magic

The thing about our books is that they are all, in their way, a blend of elven philosophy and elven magic. And this is surely in keeping with the nature of our lives and our lifestyle as elves in which magic is integral and a part of everything we do. You could say that as a people we don't tend to separate the spiritual from the mundane aspects of life but live our elven lives holistically as much as possible. Although, for the elven while the moral aspects of life are very important and infuse all that we do, we are less inclined to think of ours'elves as spiritual people than as magical people. We are not so interested in being thought of as holy as being seen as enchanting and we attempt to make our lives and our interactions with others as magical and wondrous as we possibly can.

That being said, there are some of our books that are more specially geared toward magic in its various forms, particularly in the practical as well as the philosophical aspects of elven magic. The most prominent of these is surely *The Book of Elven*

Magick, vols. one and two. These books not only have a great deal concerning our philosophy of elven magic but are especially geared to those of our kindred who may do or are interested in Wicca, Witchcraft and Western Ceremonial Magick for we have what we might call template ceremonies or rituals that one can use or adapt for one's own magical designs and purposes.

But we also have other books that have spells for practical use in them. We especially recommend *Elven Geomancy: an Ancient Oracle of the Elven Peoples for Divination and Spell Casting*. This book is not only a re-imagining of the art of Geomancy but is designed as a book of magic as well. This book is, of course, as the word -mancy denotes a book of Divination and can surely be used as such. However, if you were to ask the oracle what magic should I do to deal with this or that situation or person or to attain this or that thing, the oracle would reply by giving you a series of movements/mundras and spells/mantras that could be pieced together as a mini-spell/ritual/enchantment that you might use to obtain your stated intention.

The Elven Book of Dreams, while also an oracle, has 360 spell chants in it that can be used for one's magic. Also *The Elven Book of Powers: Using the Tarot for Magical Wish Fulfillment* is designed to be used for magic that involves the Tarot cards, not thrown out for divination so much as for spellcasting. Somewhat reminiscent of novel *The Greater Trumps* by Charles Williams, who was one of Tolkien's inner circle of friends and writers.

And, of course, there is *An Elfin Book of Spirits* that has 360 elf friendly spirits that can be summoned to aid one in one's magic. We have called quite a few of these ours'elves over the last forty years and have found the process most successful and rewarding. Also, if you are looking for guidance for your own life you may wish to evoke one of *The Shining Ones*, particularly the one that is associated with your own birthday (see our book *The Shining Ones: The Elfin Spirits That Guide You According to Your Birth Date And The Evolutionary Lessons They Offer*). These are beings that would be equivalent to Angels in elven cosmology.

We could go on like this for some time for, as we indicated, our books are filled with elfin magic but while we have these books to assist ours'elves and our kindred, mostly we try to inspire our elfin kin to create their own elvish magic, hoping that in doing so they will in turn nurture and inspire us.

❧

What book of yours is best if I'm interested in ... ? Part 2: Elven Philosophy

You can find bits of Elven Philosophy in all of our books. Even our cookbook has tidbits of elven philosophy in it, particularly about how to adapt traditional recipes to make them healthier, more to your individual taste and thus more elven. For we elves are all about catering to the natures and needs of all our kindred, as best we are able.

Our sisters of the Elf Queen's Daughters were of a different mind as far as that goes. They were ever seeking to create a group mind, a merging of individuals into a harmonious whole and thus as they often said they didn't *agree to disagree* but *agreed to agree*. But we Silver Elves, having raised two wonderful but very different and distinct elfin children, learned to seek out each one's needs and interests, as an ancient Chinese Physician would look at the needs of the body of the individual sHe was treating, and deal with what they wanted, needed and what was in their best interests.

Thus if you were among the Elf Queen's Daughters you would eat what was served. Or really, what was served was what was available and you could eat it or not. They didn't force one to eat what was offered, but they always urged one to be as adaptable as possible while giving up or limiting one's preferences and aversions. When Zardoa first stayed with the Fox River Elves, a vortex of the EQD, he'd never eaten eggs that weren't baked in a cake or bread or whatever. Melryn expressed to him the notion that he might profit by opening hims'elf up a little and, being impressed by her personality as so many were, he listened to her. Today, due to this experience expanding his diet to include eggs, he does eat omelets, which he had never done previously in his life, although he does like to have ketchup on them to hide the taste. But while we Silver Elves agree, in essence, with the wisdom of this philosophy, we still see and support the value of individual tastes. Often one's body instinctually knows what is best for it. That's why small children have some rather strong opinions on what they won't eat and often have a few staples they rely upon. We, for the most part, unless the food they choose is utterly unhealthy, honor that instinctual choice.

So, as you can see, elven philosophy is pretty much in all of our writing. It is interlaced with everything, which is also the way we educated our children by mixing what we needed to teach them with everyday life and everything they were interested in and encountered. In that way, for our male elfin child particularly, videos games were a great basis for arousing interest. As we have already pointed out, video games are surely the greatest educational tool thus far invented. For adults (a word we really don't much care for, instead we'd say more mature elfin) sex and romance are surely the greatest educational tools and inspiration for learning.

However, if you are looking for books that are dedicated to elven philosophy, particular the philosophy of the Seelie Elves, the elves of light, we have a number of books that will fill the bill. There is, first and foremost, what must be one of our most popular books *Through The Mists Of Faerie: A Magical Guide to the Wisdom Teachings of the Ancient Elven*. There is also another book of ours that many people have expressed as a favorite on elven philosophy and as a good beginning book to read in our collection: *The Elven Way: The Magical Path of the Shining Ones*. And we also suggest one of our favorites, *Liber Aelph: Words of Guidance from the Silver Elves to our Magical Children*. A number of people seem to think that this is a children's books, which it isn't but rather a book for our mature children, which is to say our children grown up, and those who are yet to come.

And for those who wish to understand our view of Cosmology and our place within the Universe and the evolution of being, we particularly recommend *Faerie Unfolding: The Cosmic Expression of the Divine Magic*.

But really, dear kin, you can find our philosophy in everything we write and do, for our lives do illuminate our elven philosophy. And with that we send you bright elven blessings and wish you a glorious day and a wondrous night to come.

ଛ

What book of yours is best if I'm interested in...?
Part 3: Elven Lifestyle

As we've stated elsewhere, various kindred who have just found us often write and ask us which of our books we'd recommend when one is starting on the elven path or just becoming acquainted with our works. Of course, we'd like to say, "All of them," but what we do usually reply is that it depends upon the individual's interests. Are they interested in Elven Philosophy particularly, or Divination, or Practical Elven Magic? What would serve them best is always the question that is in our own minds and hearts and the truth is only they know the actual answer to that. If they've come to us to tell them what they should think, feel or do, they've definitely come to the wrong elves.

In a sense, that is the Elven Lifestyle, which is to say thinking for ones'elf, being the master of one's own actions and being true to one's deep inner feelings, and from that creating one's own eald or demesne of Elfin and becoming the elf one knows ones'elf to be living the elven way. Taking care of one's life and one's elven destiny is what being an elf is all about individually. And connecting with and nurturing and sharing love with one's kindred is essentially our collective aspiration. We ever seek to create a realm where love reigns and magic interweaves all things, which really, once when one comes to understand the true nature of the Universe, one also understands is what life is all about.

For the developing elven individual, some of our philosophy books can be quite illuminating, particularly *The Elven Way* and *Liber Aelph*. But for those interested, as so many are, in group energy and the ideas concerning creating our own nation, country, tribes, bands, vortexes, etc., our book *The United States of Elfin: Imagining a More Elven Style of Government* particularly speaks to this possibility and aspiration.

But for books of a more individual nature that speak of the elven lifestyle, we have some that many have told us are germane in this regard, although they are, like most things elven, more in the way of hints and suggestions than actual directives or admonitions. Especially, we have our book on elven manners and courtesy and how to interact with both our kindred and also how one might engage with the world at large, entitled *What An Elf Would Do: A Magical Guide to the Manners and Etiquette of the Faerie Folk*. It is, we warn you, a bit tongue in cheek at times, as all our writing is at certain moments. We do have a tendency to gently tease the normal folk. But one must be very careful in doing so for they take themselves very seriously and they can be dangerous when they feel disrespected, although they are at the same time very keen to disrespect others and for their own part do not hesitate to ridicule our elven identity.

And many have told us they enjoy our book *Elf Quotes: A Collection of Over 1000 Ancient Elven Sayings and Wise Elfin Koans by the Silver Elves about Magic and the Elven Way*, which is even more prone to hints and suggestions. We endeavor to create a new elven saying every day that we publish on our Facebook "like" page *Elf Sayings of the Silver Elves*. And for those who are interested in regular but small doses of elven healing and humor on a daily basis, you are welcome to join us there.

But also you should know, in both our books and in conversation (and you are welcome to contact us on Facebook private messenger), we do our best to answer all the questions that our kindred ask of us as best we may and to help them with whatever issues they may be encountering as an elfae in the world. Although, again, often our answers amount to what do you think? What would you really like to do? What do you feel is best for you? And trust your own true s'elf.

❧

What book of yours is best if I'm interested in ... ? Part 4: Divination

We love divination. We love reading the tarot cards and tarot like decks. We love the *I Ching* and other oracles. We just do and always have. Which is why a number of our books are dedicated to divination both directly and indirectly. Thus we have our own rune book based upon our own elven rune creations *The Book of Elven Runes: A Passage Into Faerie* and we have our *The Voice of Faerie: Making Any Tarot Deck Into an Elven Oracle* in which you can apply to any tarot deck and many tarot-like decks to turn them into elven decks by giving the cards meaning and interpretation from an elvish point of view. A great deal of what we do is to look at the world and go, well if they were elven how would they see the world, or if this was written from an elven perspective what would it say, which in our experience changes nearly everything and makes it anew, better and more magical. But then, we are elves, so of course we would think that.

For instance, we took the process and technique of Geomancy and expanded and developed it and gave it our own interpretation, also making it so one could use the oracle to find a simple spell casting that comes as a result of one's question in our *Elven Geomancy: An Ancient Oracle of the Elfin Peoples for Divination and Spell Casting*. This is sort of multitasking, elven style. We often like our books to have a philosophic and practical magical aspect to them. In our lives we are ever doing bits of magic here and there, ad hoc, off the cuff and impromptu as need and circumstance demand, or in many cases implore, and we often have elfin magic in our minds anyway. We think about magic as much as some folks think about sex (and honestly to the elven mind, sex and magic are very interrelated) or some folks think about money.

Of course, our book *The Elven Book of Changes: A Magical Interpretation of the I Ching* is a favorite of ours, but this is so primarily because we love and respect it as an oracle so much. We've been doing it everyday for over forty years and it has been our faithful companion and mentor and has guided us through numerous difficult periods and adventures. It can always be relied upon to help one in a crisis, which is why we recommend it for all our kindred in the elven form we have written or nearly any other that one may relate to. If you want to hear the voice of the ancestors and get true guidance and sagely advice from them, the *I Ching* is a good way to go about it. Our version merely removes the patriarchal cultural bias that is in so many versions, as well as interpreting it from an elven point of view, which also means with a magical outlook.

On the other hand, we created *The Elven Star Oracle: A System of Divination for Star Enchanters* that is an unique elven oracle and so if you are looking for something different, something that is in that sense completely elven that incorporates the Elven Star, or as some folks call it, the Faerie Star, then this is a good oracle to check out. Sometimes we know our kindred hunger for something that is completely our own.

But there is also our book *The Shining Ones: The Elfin Spirits That Guide You According to Your Birth Date And The Evolutionary Lessons They Offer* that is both a book of magic for connecting with the Shining Ones, the higher spirits that guide and protect us, but could also be used as an oracle by asking a question and seeing what Shining One you received in response. In fact, our *An Elfin Book of Spirits: Evoking the Beneficent Power of Faerie* can also be used in the same way. One could if one wished look through the book and pick a spirit that seemed to best suit one's needs, but these elves love to throw a series of stones that picks the spirit for us and in this way we are often challenged in thinking about why we got a particular spirit for the need we had in mind. This, however, might be confusing for some folks, but we are practiced at making these sorts of connections and enjoy the process of doing so. Plus, the spirits have always proven in the long run to be the right spirit for the job. We expect a certain amount of faith is required here, but ours is a faith based upon experience. We have seen the magic work and have faith that it will continue to do so.

What book of yours is best if I'm interested in ...? Part 5: The Elf Queen's Daughters

We were awakened by the Elf Queen's Daughters. Or perhaps we should say it was due to our relationship with the Elf Queen's Daughters that we first awakened. They didn't actually do anything special to instigate this awakening beyond being their own wonderful s'elves. In fact, Zardoa had been married to an elf maiden a number of years before he first encountered the Elf Queen's Daughters but that relationship, while deeply felt, did not awaken him to the realization of his own elven nature. His time had just not come as yet. Still, his relationship with her was a clear and early indication of the nature of his being. She would fade in time, finding no support in the world for her elfin nature, as is unfortunately still the case with so many of our kindred, while he would be awakened for the rest of his life.

The Elf Queen's Daughters were an influence in the pagan community of the mid 1970's. Their *Elf Magic Mail*, the contents of which we have recreated in our two books of that title with additional commentary about our own experience, touched the lives of numerous individuals around the country and even as far as France where a brother who once came to visit us lived. He was a quite amazing and knowledgeable magician with whom we corresponded for years. He produced these incredible posters about occult lore and would send them to us regularly. We still have many of them in our treasures.

The Elf Queen's Daughters were friends with many of those who were significant in the pagan movement at that time, such as Oberon and Morninglory Zell Ravenheart, and many of the letters of *The Elf Magic Mail* (they sent out three of these every week for a couple of years) were published in the early version of the *Green Egg* magazine. They also knew Alison Harlow who helped found the Covenant of the Goddess, and Z. Budapest of the Dianic Witches and many others.

After a couple of years, they abandoned their public role and withdrew in seclusion, leaving the publication of the Elf Magic Mail to our sister Loriel, who for her part, she has told us, felt overwhelmed by the prospect at the time and just couldn't do it. As it was, a number of years later, we began their publication again, at first with the help of another sister of the Elf Queen's Daughters named Tasa, and now called them *The Magical Elven Love Letters* (see our three books of that same name, vols. 1, 2 & 3) and carried them on in a rather whimsical schedule, which means whenever we got around to it, for the next three decades, first by snail mail and then, eventually by email.

However, while the Elf Queen's Daughters faded from public view, their exploration into the esoteric and the occult continued and does continue. We lived with them for about a month and a half in 1979 and participated in a sorcerer's group they had established from 1995 to 2001 regularly traveling to their home, spending the weekend and doing what elves and sorcerer's do when they get together. Which is, of course, sorcery.

In 2008, we migrated to Hawaii, however, our relationship with our sisters of the Elf Queen's Daughters continued and continues today. We published our correspondence with them from that period in four books entitled *Magic Talks: Being a Correspondence Between The Silver Elves and the Founders of The Elf Queen's Daughters*, *Sorcerers' Dialogues: A Further Correspondence Between The Silver Elves and the Founders of The Elf Queen's Daughters*, *Discourses on High Sorcery: Continuing Correspondence Between The Silver Elves and the Founders of The Elf Queen's Daughters*, and *Ruminations on Necromancy: More Correspondence Between The Silver Elves and the Founders of The Elf Queen's Daughters*. These four books are truly a course that combines a unique elven perception on topics such as Esoteric Buddhism, soul evolution and incarnation, the cyclic universe, the Shining Ones and the supra-dimensional awareness, mayavirupas as a bodily form for faerie kind and for future humanity, the meaning of the seven rays and the adoption of the seven pointed elven star, all from an elven point of view. And this series also includes diverse discussions about elven magic and culture, telepathy, Tolkien, sorcery and shamanistic necromancy. These discussions are a synthesis of ideas that you absolutely will not read anywhere else, as the Elf Queen's Daughters and the Silver Elves combine various views of ancient wisdom into a unique perception of the world of magic.

Also, we would like to mention that members of the Elf Queen's Daughters family come to visit us here in Hawaii about every six months or so; and also our ancient sister, although she still looks as young as she ever did, Loriel visits us from time to time. But the greatest relationship we have with these kindred of ours has always been in our dreams. They have appeared in our dreams over the last 40+ years many, many times. More than any other person and continue to do so. For in our dreams we are ever connected and in the Dreaming we shall ever be one, upon the wing.

What about the accusation that the Silver Elves books are a mish-mash of cultural appropriation?

We recently had an individual write to us on Facebook and accused our books, among other things, of being a mish-mash of cultural appropriation. However, before we could reply to his comment he apparently realized he had contradicted himself in his long rant and he deleted his own comments. But, we'd like to reply to them anyway because although we think his observations are opinions really since he hadn't actually read our books nor knew us personally in any way (including our cultural background), they are accusations worth considering.

As to the idea that our books are a mish mash that is surely true. We take everything we encounter, from every culture we encounter and filter it through the lens of our elf sight. We look at the world at large much in that way that we view Elfin, that it is one place with many unique people, individuals and cultures but that these things and beings are not really separate but instead merely variations of the one, rather like a huge box of crayons. We elves wish to use all the crayons available when we color our world, not just a few. And when people tell us we can only use the blue or green but not the red or yellow or other varieties, then we look at them as though they are crazy, which they are.

We once had a friend come visit us, who was really quite impressive. She was Jewish and had escaped the Nazis in

Germany and saved herself and her children by fleeing to the Dominican Republic (since it was the only country in the world that would accept her). She was an old witch and went to a Covenant of the Goddess convention with us. One day, during her visit, as we were driving along in our car she saw our, at the time, three year old daughter coloring a drawing of an apple and she was making it purple. Our witch friend told us that we needed to compel her to color it red in order to teach her that apples are usually red and we just laughed at her and told her it was our daughter's imagination at work and she could color it any color she desired, as far as we were concerned. We had no doubt that she would in the future learn the colors apples tend to come in. Elves are not fond of having our imaginations limited, even by what some folks perceive of as reality.

We've written about cultural appropriation in a couple of our books but let us say that as elves and thus being the oldest folk, according to lore and legend, and being the hidden folk of nearly every people in the world, we feel we have the right to observe any culture we choose, since they all originally came from elves in one way or another or replaced us in our lands. So we take what they offer and view it from an elven perspective as well as transform it, hopefully making it better by doing so, and in a sense 'elfinizing' it. We actually believe everyone has that right.

What we don't believe in is taking something and making something wicked out of it. We don't mind that the faeries took our seven pointed elven star and call it the faerie star, since they are doing this in a loving and positive way. It would be nice if they knew where they got it from, but alas, forgetfulness is the way of the world. However, when the Nazis took the wonderful Hindu symbol of the swastika and used it to promote their wicked agenda, that we object to. Now whenever most people in the world see the swastika they think of Nazis and skinheads and hate and prejudice, instead of the spiral galaxy and spiritual energy it truly represents.

We once knew a woman of Hispanic heritage who was married to a gentleman of Chinese lineage, and she was the high priestess of a Celtic witchcraft coven she had founded. Now, those who are against cultural appropriation would say that she should have a coven based upon Hispanic or Spanish magic but her spirit and soul drew her to Celtic witchcraft. From an elven point of view, this woman, despite her currently genetic heritage had been a Celt in a previous lifetime and still carried that spirit within her and had every right, to our minds, to have whatever type of coven her heart and imagination, her soul and her spirit, drew her toward.

For these elves, all magic is one. It may manifest in a variety of ways and traditions around the world, but at its heart it is one magic and all magic stems from it and all magic wielders have the right to study magic in all of its forms. Saying that we can only write about magic from the culture that we are genetically descended from is ridiculous as far as these elves are concerned. That would be like saying that Western doctors can only study or do Western style medicine and Chinese doctors can only do ancient Chinese medicine and this is just patently ludicrous. Medicine does not belong to one people or culture, it belongs to all people and so does magic.

"Elves view criticism as only being valid when it promotes creativity. Otherwise, they say it is no more significant than spitting into a blazing fire."

Are all The Silver Elves' books unique and original writing?

While most all of our books are written as unique and completely original bodies of work, a few are what we would call "reimagining" of other works. For instance, *The Elven Book of Changes*: When we were first awakened by the Elf Queen's Daughters in the 70s, they taught us how to do the *I Ching*, which we've spoken of in another earlier section in this book at length. We had actually done the Ching previously but had no idea how to draw the lines and didn't understand the use of the Ching sticks to get the oracle. (They also, by the way, taught us how to construct a basic astrological chart.) We have been doing the *I Ching* everyday, at least once a day (more if we are facing difficulties or have an important decision to make), since then for over forty years. However, as much as we've attempted to inspire our kindred to use the *I Ching*, for it is a really great oracle, very few have taken it up. One of the primary objections we've heard over the years, particularly from our sisters, was how irritating the Patriarchal bias was, as well as the ancient Chinese cultural bias in which women took care of the home and children and the man was in charge of the family. Hearing the *I Ching* talk about the "superior man" over and over just drove them away from it. So we decided that we needed to create an Elven I Ching (*The Elven Book of Changes*) that would look at life from an elven perspective, which means in part that it has no gender bias in it and promotes the development of all our kindred.

Another of our books, *The Elven Book of Dreams*, is also a reimagining. We love Dane Rudhyar's book *The Astrological*

Mandala, which has 360 (one for each degree of the Zodiac) dream symbols in it. We used this book for years as a supplementary oracle but found most of the dream symbols to be quite mundane and evocative of normal culture. We wanted a version that was about elves and magic. We decided to create a book that was structurally similar, which is to say one that had 360 dreams in it, only these were elven dreams and dream fragments that Zardoa had and wrote down for over 30 years, until he collected enough and began interpreting them. We also added 360 spells to the book so that it has elven philosophy in it as well as being filled with practical elven magic. While the structure of the book is similar to Rudhyar's the contents are utterly original.

When we think of repackaging rather than original books, we think of the James Bond tarot deck that was issued with the movie *Live and Let Die* and then a few years later repackaged as *the Tarot of the Witches*, and is still available under that title. That is repackaging, same contents, different packaging. Our books, on the other hand, are all original elven views of the world.

This brings us to another question we have been asked (which was not really presented to us in the form of a question but more of an accusation) that we will address here: Do we only write our books for money? First, if we wanted money, we wouldn't be going around telling people we are elves. We've had housemates and friends who have urged us to write our books for a wider audience, make them more New Age in a general fashion and we have always resisted doing so. Money has never been the primary motivation for these elves, although, we are not at all opposed to our books becoming a financial success (are you listening spirits?).

The truth about why we write our books is first and foremost that we searched about for books on elven magic and the only thing we found were novels, which is not bad. Novels can be quite inspiring for elven magic. In fact, our entire culture was hidden in myth, lore and faerie tales for ages in order to preserve it from destruction. But of elven magic and philosophy there was nothing. So we decided that if such books didn't exist, we had an obligation as elven enchanters, wizards and magicians to create them. So we did.

But curiously, and by the way, or perhaps on the way, we discovered that we really enjoy creating these books about elven philosophy and culture. This is perhaps a bonus for us. A bit of magic gifted to us by the Shining Ones. But in truth this joy we take in creating these books has become our primary motivation in writing them. But then, that just makes sense for elves, doesn't it.

Why do you use the royal "we" when writing?

When we used to post to Elven Listserves in the 90s, we often had individuals who would ask us, usually with a touch of hostility and a challenging tone, about why we used the *Royal We* when writing. We explained to them that we were not necessarily using the *Royal We* but were in fact a family of elves and thus were using the pronoun, *we*, correctly as far as we could tell, and honestly although we were raised, or is that reared, speaking English, it has always seemed a foreign language to us. But we are fairly certain that when a letter or correspondence, which for the most part our writings really are, a sort of love letter and correspondence with and to our kindred, is sent from more than one person that *we* is the proper pronoun to use.

And to our minds when we write our books or in fact correspond with our kindred, we are writing not only for ours'elves but for our entire elven family and all those kindred of ours who happen to agree with us. In part, this tendency perhaps derives from our time when we were part of the Elf Queen's Daughters back in the mid 1970's. In that sisterhood, who published three letters of the *Elf Magic Mail* (see our two books of that title that have the contents of those original letters) each week and sent them out by snail mail and also wrote to hundreds of elves and elf friends via personal correspondence around the United States and in Europe, it was quite common not only for various members to contribute a sentence or paragraph to one of the letters of the *Elf Magic Mail*, but to answer correspondence individually for and as the group.

We remember when we first went to visit our sisters (and brothers, but in the EQD we were all considered sisters) Melryn and the other three elves of that vortex had to go off to work for the day and left us at the vortex to answer letters that had been sent to them. They had a metal filing cabinet full of correspondence both old and pending and Melryn said to us to just pick any that called to us and to write to them on their behalf. So we did. One of the letters we particularly liked was from a French magician with whom we continued correspondence from our own vortex in Southern Illinois, where we called ours'elves the Elves of the Southern

Woodlands. A year or so later, he traveled from France to visit us.

The sisters used to say, "We are of One Heart and One Mind," and they meant that rather literally, that they were so close psychically that it was in certain ways hard to tell them apart. They functioned from their point of view like a flock of birds and had the psychic interconnection of porpoises and dolphins. Andruil once said to us: "We all write the Elf Magic Mail and no one can tell which of us wrote what."

We remember one particular personal letter these elves received from Arwen and Elanor, who founded the Elf Queen's Daughters, in which they wrote to us saying, "Speak for us." And they meant that quite literally. By those simple words they authorized us to represent them and the sisterhood, which is in part why a few years later in 1979, after they had relinquished writing *The Elf Magic Mail,* we began our own letters *The Magical Elven Love Letters,* which were essentially a continuation of those letters and which eventually evolved into our books (see our books *The Magical Elven Love Letters,* volume 1, 2, & 3).

At the same time, it should be noted that all elves are royal and we could each and everyone of us use the *Royal We* if we so choose. However, it is important to understand that in Elfin, royalty is not a position of authority, except over one's own s'elf, but a recognition of one's essential value as a soulful spirit. Just as Aleister Crowley wrote in *the Book of the Law* that, "Every Man and Woman is a Star," so too is every elf of royal heritage with the right/rite to rule hir own life and direct hir destiny as sHe see fit.

☙

About the Authors

The Silver Elves, Zardoa and Silver Flame, are a family of elves who have been living and sharing the Elven Way since 1975. They are the authors of 41 books on magic and enchantment, available on Amazon internationally, and your local bookstore, including:

The Book of Elven Runes: A Passage Into Faerie;

The Magical Elven Love Letters, volume 1, 2, and 3;

An Elfin Book of Spirits: Evoking the Beneficent Powers of Faerie;

Caressed by an Elfin Breeze: The Poems of Zardoa Silverstar;

Eldafaryn: True Tales of Magic from the Lives of the Silver Elves;

Arvyndase (Silverspeech): A Short Course in the Magical Language of the Silver Elves;

The Elven Book of Dreams: A Magical Oracle of Faerie;

The Book of Elven Magick: The Philosophy and Enchantments of the Seelie Elves, Volume 1 & 2;

What An Elf Would Do: A Magical Guide to the Manners and Etiquette of the Faerie Folk;

The Elven Tree of Life Eternal: A Magical Quest for One's True S'Elf;

Magic Talks: On Being a Correspondence Between the Silver Elves and the Elf Queen's Daughters;

Sorcerers' Dialogues: A Further Correspondence Between the Silver Elves and the Founders of the Elf Queen's Daughters;

Discourses on High Sorcery: More Correspondence Between the Silver Elves and the Founders of the Elf Queen's Daughters;

Ruminations on Necromancy: Continuing Correspondence Between the Silver Elves and the Founders of the Elf Queen's Daughter;

The Elven Way: The Magical Path of the Shining Ones;

The Book of Elf Names: 5,600 Elven Names to Use for Magic, Game Playing, Inspiration, Naming One's Self and One's Child, and as Words in the Elven Language of the Silver Elves;

Elven Silver: The Irreverent Faery Tales of Zardoa Silverstar;

An Elven Book of Ryhmes: Book Two of the Magical Poems of Zardoa Silverstar;

The Voice of Faerie: Making Any Tarot Deck Into an Elven Oracle;

Liber Aelph: Words of Guidance from the Silver Elves to our Magical Children;

The Shining Ones: The Elfin Spirits That Guide You According to Your Birth Date and the Evolutionary Lessons They Offer;

Living the Personal Myth: Making the Magic of Faerie Real in One's Own Personal Life;

Elf Magic Mail, The Original Letters of the Elf Queen's Daughters with Comentary by the Silver Elves, Book 1 and 2;

The Elves of Lyndarys: A Magical Tale of Modern Faerie Folk;

The Elf Folk's Book of Cookery: Recipes For a Delighted Tongue, a Healthy Body and a Magical Life;

Faerie Unfolding: The Cosmic Expression of the Divine Magic;

The Elements of Elven Magic: A New View of Calling the Elementals Based Upon the Periodic Table of Elements;

The Keys to Elfin Enchantment: Mastery of the Faerie Light Through the Portals of Manifestation;

Elf Quotes: A Collection of Over 1000 Ancient Elven Sayings and Wise Elfin Koans by The Silver Elves About Magic and The Elven Way;

The United States of Elfin Imagining A More Elven Style of Government; and

Elven Geomancy: An Ancient Oracle of the Elfin Peoples for Divination and Spell Casting.

Creating Miracles In the Modern World: The Way Of the Elfin Thaumaturge

The Silver Elves have had various articles published in *Circle Network News Magazine* since 1986 and have given out over 6,000 elven names to interested individuals in the Arvyndase language, with each elf name having a unique meaning specifically for that person. They are also interviewed and mentioned numerous times in *Not In Kansas Anymore* by Christine Wicker (Harper San Francisco, 2005) and in *A Field Guide to Otherkin* by Lupa (Megalithica Books, 2007), and are discussed in Nikolay Lyapanenko's recent book *The Elves From Ancient Times To Our Days: The Magical Heritage of "Starry People" and their Continuation Into the Modern World* (2017) that gives a detailed account of their involvement in the Elven Movement since 1975. Also, an interview with the Silver Elves is included in Emily Carding's recent popular book *Faery Craft* (Llewellyn Publications, 2012).

The Silver Elves understand the world as a magical or miraculous phenomena, and that all beings, by pursuing their own true path, will become whomever they truly desire to be. You are welcome to visit their website at **http://silverelves.angelfire.com**, visit their blog site at https://thesilverelves.blogspot.com on the Elven Way and also their blog site on Elven Lifestyle, Magic and Enchantment at https://silverelves.wordpress.com, and join them on Facebook with the names as "Michael J. Love (Zardoa of The SilverElves)" and "Martha Char Love (SilverFlame of The SilverElves)."

Made in the USA
Middletown, DE
27 January 2018